NATURE'S
Healing Spirit

Real Life Stories to Nurture the Soul

Sheri McGregor
plus 33 accomplished writers

Sowing Creek Press
San Marcos, California

Sowing Creek Press
711 Center Drive, Ste. 105, Box 129
San Marcos, CA 92069
Email: info@sowingcreekpress.com
www.sowingcreekpress.com

Nature's Healing Spirit: Real Life Stories to Nurture the Soul/
Sheri McGregor—1st ed.
ISBN: 978-0-9973522-2-1 (print)
ISBN: 978-0-9973522-3-8 (E-book)

Library of Congress Control Number: 2018900834

Book cover and interior design by Lorie DeWorken, mindthemargins.com

Publisher's Cataloging-In-Publication Data
(Prepared by The Donohue Group, Inc.)

Names: McGregor, Sheri, 1961- author, compiler, editor.
Title: Nature's healing spirit : real life stories to nurture the soul /
    Sheri McGregor ; plus 33 accomplished writers.
Description: 1st ed. | San Marcos, California : Sowing Creek Press, [2018]
    | Summary: "This true anthology joins the benefits of nature to the
    joy of reading. Nature's Healing Spirit: Real Life Stories to Nurture the
    Soul provides a window into the personal lives of 34 people who find
    physical, mental and spiritual healing in nature."--Provided by publisher.
Identifiers: ISBN 9780997352221 (print) | ISBN 9780997352238 (ebook)
Subjects: LCSH: Nature, Healing power of--Literary collections. | Nature,
    Healing power of--Anecdotes. | Nature--Religious aspects--Literary
    collections. | Nature--Religious aspects--Anecdotes. | Spiritual healing--
    Literary collections. | Spiritual healing--Anecdotes.
Classification: LCC BL65.N35 M34 2018 (print) | LCC BL65.N35 (ebook) |
    DDC 202/.12/02--dc23

Dedication

For readers seeking respite for the soul.

May you find it in these pages, in the great outdoors,
or by taking notice of the tiniest of nature's wonders.

Table of Contents

Acknowledgments

Thank you to those who submitted their stories to this anthology, and especially to those whose essays were chosen for inclusion. Your enthusiasm, patience, and professionalism is appreciated.

And thank you also to people who take notice and find joy in the natural world. *You* are part of nature. Your healing spirit reverberates around the globe.

A Note from Sheri McGregor
The How and Why Behind the Book

Take a breath and settle into a favorite spot as you begin this book where everyday life intersects with the natural world. Thirty-four writers share their experiences and come away stronger, wiser, and happier.

When I began reading the more than 300 submissions in early 2017, I would pull up a chair near my small pond where the lilies spread yellow and pink petals to the morning sun. As I set my pages on the low wall of the garden bed behind me, masses of crane flies rose in a wave of clumsy, transparent wings and dangling legs. They would fall like drab confetti into the dewy grass growing among the rosemary and sage. In the pecan and pine trees, collared-doves fluttered about, gathering in the warm, pre-spring air. This invasive dove species, with a shrill call, like the breathy notes of an accordion, drawn out and repeated, has settled here. The collared-doves have multiplied, and live peacefully alongside the native mourning doves with their soft coos.

Outdoors at my semi-rural, inland California home seemed the perfect setting to enjoy the stories. I couldn't know my year

1

would soon grow chaotic, and the process of reading and choosing among the submissions would stretch through the seasons. Now, having seen nearly a year filled with family complications, household repairs, and various setbacks, I know that reading about these experiences in nature couldn't have come at a better time.

This wasn't the first time the resilience of the natural world has nurtured my own. I have often turned to the solace of quiet spaces—in the woods, on grassy hilltops, or in the cool swath of shade looking up at sunlight filtered through the leaves of a tree—to still myself in times of trouble, chaos, or despair.

Fifteen years ago, my son was in a serious car accident. During the time we were struggling with his recovery, I had just finished writing a local hiking guide when a firestorm hit. Many of the trails described in the work went up in smoke. For the guide's accuracy, I re-hiked the areas burned in the season's firestorms that changed the landscape. Witnessing the way plants and animals adapted to the devastation, helped me to also heal. Masses of poodle-dog bush with its showy purple blooms sprang up in sunny spots once canopied in darkness by towering incense cedar trees. On charred old oaks, fresh new leaves burst forth in wreaths, circling the blackened trunks and limbs. Bobcats and deer walked in full view, on wildlife trails once hidden by the understory of tangled brush. Seeing nature's resilience sparked my own buoyant spirit, and gave me faith that my son would also make a full recovery. As it turns out, nature's healing spirit mirrored his. You'll read a little about my son's recovery in my essay, "Swimming," included in *Nature's Healing Spirit: Real Life Stories to Nurture the Soul.*

A few years later, at a Costco book-signing after the second edition of that hiking guide was released, an elderly man with a cane came by the table. He stood reading a few passages of the book, and then told me he was going to purchase it. "I can't get out in nature like I used to," he said, lifting his cane. "But I like all your descriptions. It'll be fun for me to read about all the birds and plants and trees."

During the next several years, as two more of my hiking guides came out and a third edition of the first one, I heard that same sentiment repeated. People enjoyed reading about the flora and fauna almost as much as getting out in it. And I could relate.

Part of my joy in creating those guides was re-experiencing those wilderness treks, and savoring every moment once again when writing about them. I took great joy in bringing to life through words the tiniest wonders. Like the way a gray cicada blends in with leaf litter on a mountain trail, or a dragonfly's thin body and transparent wings make it nearly invisible as it rests, like a drab flower, atop dried grass at the edge of a pond. The sky looks bluer when seen from the dim forest floor, framed by treetops. Moss and lichen in hues of green and gray map out intricate patterns on a boulder's surface. Frogs squeak out an echoing chorus when startled—*splish-splash*—into the water of a natural pond.

When the mind is gentled by these sights and sounds, and the *busy*-ness and stress is left behind, solutions seem to fall into place. In the serenest of moments, with a woodpecker's gentle tap in the distance, the lull-a-bye hush of a rustling meadow breeze, or the dense sound of stillness on a desert trail, the puzzles of life can become so clear. Decisions that have been wrestled with and pored over simplify. Relationships can mend, deepen, and bloom.

Knowing this firsthand, and hearing the same from countless others, I started thinking about a book like this—the first in a series

Positive Effects

Numerous studies from around the world show nature's positive influence on the way people feel, think, and behave. Some of the benefits include:

- Reduced stress
- Increased creativity
- More happiness
- Enhanced capability for problem-solving
- Increased longevity

- Greater sense of connection
- Added kindness
- Lowered blood pressure and heart rate
- Faster healing
- Improvement in the symptoms of ADHD

that offers a window into people's personal lives through their connection to the natural world.

Even viewing beautiful nature scenes or sitting near potted plants has been associated with positive effects on generosity and mood. Numerous studies indicate that reading has similar benefits. This book marries nature's positive effects with those of reading. These social and psychological benefits can help with troubled relationships, too. You'll find a few essays in this collection that parallel the positive effects with the ebb and flow of a long-term marriage, parenting, or reconciling a relationship's end.

Slow down and savor these rich sensory writings. You'll venture into the ocean, meander along wooded paths, birdwatch near teeming ponds, and kayak on tranquil tributaries—always with a unique viewpoint about the way nature heals. The settings are diverse: ancient canyons in the Southwest, wooded parks connecting major cities in the East, mountains that stand sentry in the Pacific Northwest, and even your own backyard full of bugs.

Writers' Voices

Nature expresses itself in ways that are as unique as the individuals taking in its wonder. As you'll see in the pages that follow, benefits can take the form of a physical healing, a spiritual awakening, or a therapeutic blend of both. Nature connects us to the generations and rituals of our own family, the entire human family, and even to ourselves. Amid the mundane routines and crisis management of a year that went awry, I was profoundly grateful to read these artful, funny, deeply moving pieces, and walk in the writers' footsteps to find peace, inspiration, and joy.

Among the submissions, writers' voices ran the gamut from squirrels sounding in alarm to the softest raindrops falling on leaves—and everything in between. These works ranged from academic, scientific, and even horrific, all resplendent with the sights and sounds of nature as a backdrop. The writers themselves were as varied. Parents with packed schedules, students whose writing derived from MFA programs, the professors of those programs, or busy professionals in various careers. Youngsters to young adults to young octogenarians. Choosing which works to include was not an easy task.

The essays, and even a few poems, in this collection vary in tone and content. Some are straightforward and forthright. Others more literary and subtle. Some skip jubilantly into the realm of the wild. Others tread a darker path into the proverbial woods. What connects them is the nature of being human ... in the seasons of life.

Let Your Spirit Take Flight

As you read, let your spirit take flight—on the wings of snowy pelicans, a cunning crow, a moth as big as a bat, or even on the white-tipped tails of foxes leaping in the night.

Reading how the lush landscapes of the natural world connect and collide with the lives of the writers can be good medicine. Don't try to consume too much at once. Reflect upon the healing, and then consider how the stories parallel your own. What's your takeaway? Take time to fully immerse yourself in each writer's experience. Touched by nature, you're likely to emerge feeling calm and content.

As I write this introduction, the lilies in my pond are dormant. The minnows that were tiny flecks with fins and tails in the spring sunlight survived the hot days of summer when an egret came to dine, and have grown fat and rosy and sluggish. My year is closing with a crescendo of chaos, but I am hopeful. The year was a season that will soon end. A new one will begin, just as nature cycles and brings restoration.

Orca Meditation

by Lisa Lebduska

My husband Steven and I chose San Juan Island in Washington State to witness life outside—not just outside the conditioned air of the house and the fluorescence of the office, but life outside of the East Coast, of wet Connecticut and its slippery ledge. But when we arrive at the waterfront for our sea kayak wildlife tour, it looks like everyone else had the same idea.

Dozens of vacationers are on the beach. Kids, grandparents, and teens with tattoos slather on sunscreen, don hats and sunglasses, and slip their feet into plastic slippers. Each breeze carries a small whiff of suntan lotion.

Lots of guides with clipboards and faded baseball caps are standing around. One shepherds us into a small cabin, where we are shown an instructional video on kayak safety. I have kayaked only twice before, have no upper body strength, and tend to get very disoriented about such things as the right way to hold a paddle, how to cinch my lifebelt and which side to paddle on, but I resist the urge to take notes.

Soon we have learned enough for the real experience. We are led outside.

The sand is cool and pebbly; the dark water calm and very, very cold. Madronas—slim, twisting trees with orange-red bark and green foliage—line the hills overlooking the shore. It seems quiet in the trees, in the arms of their branches and down below. Quiet in the water, quiet everywhere, I think, except where our gaggle of tourists calls out to one another.

The guides each take a group and paddle out into the sea, the yellow kayaks bobbing across the waves. Steven and I are paired with an American family (mother, father and two young freckled boys) and a Dutch family (father, mother and teen brother and sister).

Our guide is Liam, a tall gangly young man with a perpetual half smile, whose beard is the same reddish shade as the madronas. He instructs us further on holding our paddles and teaches us how to put on the rubber skirt that will keep us dry. "It's easy," he says, demonstrating, as he gracefully lowers himself into the boat and snaps the skirt into place. "You just hop in."

The Dutch Mom, considerably older and larger than Liam, says everything I am thinking: "At my age and size, Liam," she tells him with a slight German accent, "one does not hop so easily."

Silently I bless her for voicing my fears, and then try to shelve my worries: *what if I mess up and tip the kayak, what if I put this thing on backward (I am always putting things on backward), what if I get so cold I have to quit, what if I have to go to the bathroom in the middle of all of this.* I am well past twelve years of age, so I do not say any of this.

I lower myself into the kayak, and my husband pushes it through the wet sand, and then hops in. We are paddling in a small pod: Liam in the lead, with the rest of us paddling behind like dutiful, confused ducks.

Once we get past a few low waves and the water smooths out, I settle down onto my seat and keep paddling. Within a few moments, I feel the gentle lapping of the water around us, and I am cradled. I am close to the water, eye level with a whole new strata of life. The land meets my gaze differently; I can feel the air coming into my lungs.

We are low and close to a world that swims beneath. There is no machinery: no radio, no leaf blowers, no chainsaws, no engines of any kind. Just human voices, some birds, the knocking of the paddles against the kayak and the sea. I realize that I am no longer fighting to block out sounds. I want to hear everything, as if I were listening to a long-lost friend telling me what she had been doing with her life.

A curious otter, all whiskers and chocolate-drop eyes, pops out, inspects us and disappears. Then he pops up again a few yards away. In the trees, crows watch and call. I feel not so much watched as watched over. Liam tells us that soon we will reach an eagle's nest, perched along a cliff.

Every so often, we hear a small splash, and if we are quick enough, we are treated to a silvery salmon leaping into the air for a damsel fly. Nature is both instantaneous and biblical in its pacing. Here, in the cradle of the kayak, I can feel both paces at once. After a time—I cannot say how long—I realize that I am not checking anything. We must simply look and look again and paddle. The more we look, the more we see.

First, the broad brush of landscape: shore and sky and sea. But then, with our focus on the same picture, details emerge: a tiny black-headed duck, bobbing expertly, tiny minnows paddling, a white thread of cloud across a deep sky. I do not feel at one with nature, but I start to merge with its rhythms. The things in my life that usually pace me—the car as I drive, the phone whenever it buzzes or rings or sings, the computer as it flashes—recede into a different part of my life.

However peaceful, we are all also keeping watch, hopeful that we will at least glimpse an Orca. We have strained to see the blowholes, the big sprays of water indicating that an orca swims beneath. But it is not until we have finished our lunch and loaded ourselves back in the boats that Liam says quite seriously, "The Orcas are coming. Raft up."

Quickly, we recall the instructions he had given us on the shore: *When I give the signal 'raft up' that means paddle together and hold hands. We need to stay close together in the event that the Orcas pass through.*

I cannot quite believe that this is happening. I have not spotted the Orcas, but I know that whales are house-sized. I cannot quite fathom that a house is there under the water.

And then, straight ahead, I see them: glistening black fins slicing through the water. By this time, we have rafted up, and I am holding tightly to the American boy in the kayak next to ours. I hear his mother tell him to relax, and I look at his face, a mix of terror and curiosity.

I think of movies and art work; illustrations from *Moby Dick*. I remember seeing the great whale hanging from the ceiling of the Museum of Natural History. *Big*, is all my mind can come up with. The fins glide across the water gently. I think of my mind, in that moment, and, while it is registering *big*, it is not registering a corresponding small for me. The approaching fins do not make me feel tiny or insignificant. I feel only calm.

I am not one with the giant creature gliding toward me, but I am its witness, a part of the same wide sky and deep, broad sea, on the same blue jewel spinning around the same sun itself moving ever outward in the same great solar system of the same starry galaxy. We move together.

The black fins head straight for us and then, noiselessly, they dip beyond our sight. I do not feel them pass underneath. They do not turn around. They disappear, across the sea. But we have moved together. This I know. This I will remember always, on the darkest of days, in the coolest lonely rooms of people.

The great, giant creatures of the sea that could have so easily wrecked us, visited instead, sensed us, gracefully allowed us a glimpse, joined us to them in a moment on the sea and then vanished.

The water stays smooth and dark.

No longer needing to "raft up," we release hands and drift slightly apart. The American mom pats her son on the shoulder, telling him he has done a good job.

Everyone starts to chatter and laugh. I trail my hand in the water to share the same droplets that have touched the whales. They are there, somewhere, I know.

We paddle back to the beachhead, wet, happy, sunburned where we missed a spot. I will replay that moment until it becomes a meditation, a mantra image of a universe in gentle motion, the kayak my cradle, the Orca my guide.

LISA LEBDUSKA teaches writing and directs the college writing program at Wheaton College in Massachusetts. Her work has appeared in such journals as *bioStories*, *Kudzu Review*, *Animal* and *Narrative*, among others. She is at her best when she is out of doors.

Pictures of Phoebes

by Gail Marlene Schwartz

June 18th

I arrive at the house and get smacked in the face with cobwebs. Choose the downstairs bedroom because the gold comforter is softest, plus I can hear the brook. The lake is icy but I swim the width, then start a fire in the woodstove. I look out the kitchen window and, sure enough, the phoebe is back, sitting on four eggs.

It's been nine months since my divorce. I've rented the cabin we used to come to, and the familiarity is strangely comforting. The terror of single life subsides, replaced with the richness of this place.

June 19th

A sunbeam wakes me. I pull back the lace tablecloth clipped up for a curtain and glance at the nest. Her feathers are deep grey, her beak long. She is surprisingly nonchalant when I open the clunky porch door and pull up a child's chair to stand on.

June 20th

Temperature is up and my skin is browning. I finish a book by the lake. At dusk I make a fire in the pit and watch bats zoom out from the eaves. I check the eggs regularly; she's patient with me tramping on and off the porch.

June 21st

I take pictures: spiders, irises, tadpoles and the phoebe.
It's going to be soon.

June 22nd

My days are full of cirrus clouds, thunderclaps, dewy grass and sandy feet. I swim and sit and write and dream. I drink my coffee down by the lake. Every time I pass through the kitchen, I glance out at the nest. She's gone a lot today, so I step up onto the chair after lunch. I gasp and let a few tears go. The nest is full of strange, embryonic beings with putty-coloured skin and white fuzz. I want to call someone. I want to share something a phone conversation can't convey.

I quietly pick up my camera and snap a picture. Pinky-white blob.

June 23rd

My devotion to the nest has quadrupled. She sits on four fragile bodies, keeping them warm. I want to ask if there's anything I can do. There is no language, no code. I can only look. And take pictures. And, just in case, I talk to her.

June 24th

Fern visits. We make oatmeal cookies and bad jokes and stay up into the blue hour. Every time I'm in the kitchen I check on them. They are definitely getting bigger, and I can now see the outlines of four separate bodies. I bring a second chair out onto the porch for Fern and make her step up to see. She looks but it's not the same.

June 25th

The babies are lifting their heads!

June 26th

The phoebe leaves the nest often to go find food, and now she's clearly irritated with me. One time I climb onto the chair, and she flies at me suddenly, a tiny grey-feathered Kamikaze. Another time I'm in the kitchen, and she hovers like a hummingbird to feed the babies, then turns and looks for me through the glass. I feel guilty, hovering as I am. She was here first.

June 27th

Their necks are thickening, and I see four beaks opening and closing, cavernous airy demands. The mother stuffs food in. These birds are all mouth.

Their eyes are still closed.

I'm still taking pictures. Bulging eyelids. Fuzzy stretching necks.

June 28th

A realization: these birds are going to fly away. I distract myself with kneading dough for a homemade Challah.

June 29th

A wing! One of them stretches and extends it, like a tiny gymnast warming up. Oil coloured feathers poke out of their skin and they're keeping their mother busy. She flies in and out, in and out, in and out. It looks exhausting but she's handling it.

June 30th

My cousins come. I want my space. The nest is overflowing with phoebes.

July 1st

My sister comes for French toast with real maple syrup. I bring a second chair out onto the porch for her and make her step up to see. She looks but it's not the same.

I'm still taking pictures. Darkening fuzz. Delicate beaks.

July 2nd

I am startled in the morning, drinking my coffee, when one of the babies flutters its wings. Maybe they need to build muscle mass before they leave home.

July 3rd

Their eyes are open!

July 4th

Feathers are filling in and the color is darker, a rich stony-blue grey, like the lake just before a storm. The fourth one is now jammed in the back. I'm concerned somebody will fall out.

I'm still taking pictures. Staring black eyes. Tilting heads.

July 5th

My vacation is almost finished. I look out the window and see only three babies. Worried, I check but don't see anybody on the porch floor. I stand up on the little chair; the gang's all here. They are fat and their feathers glisten in the soft hay-coloured light of the afternoon.

July 6th

It's my last day. They are ready to take off. I want to give them something. I tell them the world is harsh. I tell them the world is full of beauty. I tell them about the lake, about the curtain I clip up to give them privacy. I tell them how my camera lens got scratched. I tell them they'll be fine. I tell them I'll be fine.

I step out onto the porch one last time. A flurry of flapping and they're gone.

I pack.

I clean.

I cry.

I get into my car.

Empty and full at the same time, I'm ready, even excited, to go home and start creating my new life as a single person.

GAIL MARLENE SCHWARTZ' story, "Inside, Crying," was a finalist in the Malahat Review's Open Season Award for fiction, 2014; her essay, "Loving Benjamin," won Honorable Mention in *Room Magazine's* contest in 2012. Gail's work has been published in *Sunday@6*, *Poetica*, *Witty Bitches*, and *Wilde Magazine* and in anthologies *How to Expect What You're Not Expecting* (TouchWood Editions, 2013) and *Hidden Lives* (Brindle and Glass, 2012). She lives in southern Quebec with her family.

Finding My Place

by Gayla Mills

When we first arrived in Richmond, I felt that I'd never be part of it. Longing for woods and fields, I had steeled myself to living amidst pavement, glass, and buildings that blocked the sunlight. I remembered driving through the city as a girl, closing my window to keep the gritty air outside, dismayed by the billboards that distracted from the sky.

We'd be working downtown, yet I hoped to find a neighborhood nearby that didn't feel too urban. We looked on a map for patches of green and were startled by just how much was growing on the page. It would be months before I discovered on foot just how wild and extensive those green patches were.

Unlike the pristine manicured parks of the suburbs, Richmond has vast wild areas—over 500 acres—that nature has recalled. The James River is responsible for this bounty. Flowing through the middle of the city and prone to flooding, the river and its floodplains have discouraged development. Good city planning and a new-found respect for the economic draw of the river have done the rest.

It was thanks to our two puppies that I began to explore these secretive places. As the dogs' size and stamina increased, our walks progressed from city blocks to miles of unkempt trails. There were streams and waterfalls, rivers and inlets, lakes and wetlands. It's no wonder Richmond is a birder's paradise, considered one of the best places in Virginia to view unusual species. With my untrained eyes I am drawn to the larger birds—from the ducks and geese on the marshy wetlands in Forest Hill Park to the herons gliding and the eagles soaring over the James River. Woodpeckers *tap tap* above, as wrens and Carolina chickadees pass from one berry bush to the next.

The Forest Hill and James River parks are connected by Reedy Creek. One can travel between them by walking up some stone stairs and crossing a winding road. I prefer, though, to travel through one of several large culverts that allow the creek passage under Riverside Drive. When you're in the tunnels, light filters through the vines hanging down on either end, creating an eerie feeling.

On the trails, each turn brings a new mood. One bend reveals cliffs 100 feet high, their jagged reaches and clinging vegetation a welcome sight to eyes accustomed to the gentle vistas of central Virginia. The next bend and the sun hides, as the moss-covered rocks and trickling stream bask in the coolness of the tight canopy overhead. A few minutes more brings a rough-hewn meadow, with a trail cut through with wildflowers ablaze. Head down to the river, where time has carved mysterious islands, inlets, and river rock, and deposited sands and twisted branches on the shores and in the crevices. The islands can be reached by wooden bridges, exposed rocks, or simple wading. I eat blackberries in the spring and paw paws in the fall as the river glides or rages by, depending on how well it has been fed by mountain streams from the west.

Visiting these places is the high point of the day for the dogs— and for me. For them it is a time to fully engage their senses, to escape from the familiar smells of the house to the rich scents of the greater world. They greedily sniff the air, nostrils flared and tails alert, until they detect the irresistible. With a rapid 180 they flip and leap off in pursuit of a deer or squirrel or raccoon they've tracked down but can't catch. Usually, though, they sniff the earth patiently and thoroughly, investigating the details of visitors long gone, of flesh and fowl who have hidden dens and nests.

As a human I'm more drawn to the visual. An acorn cap is nestled in a fading red leaf, with pine needles scattered through the still-vivid green. At the same moment, the river rages beyond the trees, and I see the silver flashes of sunlight prancing along the froth. The watery expanse is wild and fresh, clean and brisk, and I forget that the trees mask a city behind.

Winter promises solitude. Fewer people venture out in the crisp air as it slaps the skin and transports the cries of birds in flight. But the air also carries the distant sound of cars rushing by, for the greens and browns which once hid signs of the city are composting underfoot. With houses and railroad cars exposed, the illusion that one is in the wilderness is much harder to maintain. We are in a developed place, not in the wilds of Montana or on the shores that Lewis and Clark explored.

Warm weather brings river action. Fishermen hide under the overhanging trees as they hook their prey. Runners flash by in their neon colors. Cyclists brave the rough trails on their mountain bikes. Groups of children follow their teachers. But more than anyone else, dogs come down with their people to romp and nip. Though there are long spaces in which to enjoy the parks alone, warm weather means more people are present and visible amidst the landscape.

Summer invites those with time to the shore, where I find a democratic collection of sun, water, and beer worshippers. Belle Island remains the most popular destination of the river islands east of Pony Pasture. With flat rocks as perfect for human sunbathing as they are for the birds, Belle is strewn with bikinis and picnics, solitary readers and rowdy groups. The James has Class IV rapids as it speeds around the island, so it's a favorite among rafters, kayakers, and a few foolish body surfers. Sometimes people die, mostly because they try to swim between the rocks while drunk. Belle has so much the feel of a tropical paradise that people seem to forget the river isn't tame.

Fall charms, with skies richly blued and filled with intense clouds full of feeling. Colors burst before fading. The wind picks up and makes us notice the air. Critters scurry in anticipation. Everyone runs around gathering nuts to munch on during the long cold days.

This last fall, as I walked along an autumn path with my aging dogs and felt the energy in the air, I also did my numbers. If all went well, I might have thirty or so fall seasons left. That doesn't seem like nearly enough. Only thirty? And what about those years when I'm too busy gathering nuts to notice the leaves? Will those be subtracted from my thirty?

And so, I watched more intensely as a yellowed leaf fell before me, and then landed on a spot where it would decay and merge with other fallen leaves. The years lay in a soft carpet underfoot. The land felt solid.

The parks bind me to this city. They are semi-feral, daily dying and being reborn, free and uncontrolled. Like a life well-lived, they are lined with the wrinkles of time, worn by the river and sun, friend to critters and plants of all sorts. Yet they are also marked by their daily contact with the city's people. My daily walks through the parks remind me of my own ties to the soil and the wind and the water, to the birds and the beasts and the air.

I've long forgotten my fear of a cold, asphalt landscape. Now when I think of the city, I imagine not only the life teeming on the streets and in the restaurants, but also along the banks of the river and in the woods. I know that after I'm gone, and my ashes are feeding new life in the soil, that the city and its parks will charm new people without me. And I'm okay with that.

Formerly a professor of writing, GAYLA MILLS publishes essays, reviews, and flash fiction. Her essays have appeared in *Spry*, *Prairie Wolf Press*, *Skirt!*, *The Truth about the Fact*, *Greenwoman*, *The Stylus*, *Agenda: The Magazine of Politics and Culture*, and *The Hook*. Her chapbook of personal essays, *Finite* (2012), won the RED OCHRE LiT Chapbook contest. Also a musician, Mills is working on a book about getting more from music in the second half of life. Find out more at: www.gaylamills.com

The Dinosaur Footprint

by Michael G. Smith

The refreshingly cool water feels like revival beneath the hot Utah sun. Kayakers paddle near the reservoir's boat ramp on the opposite shoreline. Behind me, the canyon's tawny sandstone rises at a thirty-degree angle. Minutes ago I hiked down its grainy surface to swim. Several breaststrokes from where it meets water, the black-ink blue belies the fact that the sloped canyon is at least twenty feet below me. Naked, I disappear into depths.

Lying in the emergency room with little command over my body, I sensed I had suffered a stroke. The day before, I had been mountain biking. That morning, I was picking tomatoes and dead-heading roses in the gardens.

Dr. Baten, a neurologist, methodically examined me. He pricked my extremities with a needle. I felt sharp stabs in my right hand and foot, but not the left. He had me bring my index fingers to my nose. My right easily found it. My left waved through the air like a wild hare. He asked me to squeeze his outstretched index fingers with both hands simultaneously. My right was much stronger than my left. I only discerned the difference when his left knuckle cracked. I could lift my right leg and touch his hand with my foot. I could not lift my left leg. He asked me to follow his moving finger with my eyes. Flickering from a nystagmus, they could not. My vision honeycombed like a fly's, vibrating copies of everything in the room made me nauseous. Light stung. I kept my eyes closed.

Surprised a 43-year-old fit male was stroked and wanting to know why, Dr. Baten said, "Tell me everything that has happened to you the past week. I calmly described twisting my neck in yoga class five nights earlier while settling into a gentle backbend I had done thousands of times. A *shearing* headache jolted me awake from a sound sleep the next night. It disappeared as quickly as rising. After mountain bike riding three days later, I felt a flu coming on. After a nap a few hours earlier, I collapsed when rising.

Combining my physical symptoms with details from the past week, Dr. Baten concluded that I had suffered an ischemic stroke in my right cerebellum. More to assembled family members than to me, he pronounced that he knew why, adding emphatically that I had a long road ahead. Unruffled, I stoically knew I had no choice but to meet the situation and its consequences with the belief all would ultimately be for the best.

I had not anticipated swimming in the Red Fleet State Park reservoir. Climbing the winding road from Vernal, Utah, I had passed the entrance to the park driving to Bozeman, Montana for my summer job doing chemistry research at Montana State University the last few years. This section of road, called the *Drive Through the Ages,* cuts through eleven geologic layers totaling one hundred and fifty million years from the Early Jurassic to the Late Cretaceous. Roadside signs mark the name of each formation, and the dinosaur and marine life that lived then. Several miles past the park entrance is a sign for a dinosaur trackway, a collection of fossilized footprints. I vowed to see them before embarking from my New Mexico home on this trip. I turn onto Donkey Flat Road. Shadowing the strata's contours, the road seems misnamed.

An information kiosk is at the trailhead. I read the signs, take a trail-description brochure and begin walking. The one-and-a-half-mile trail rises and falls as it traverses through the rust-red Navajo sandstone. Desert varnish coats the rock. Patches of deep sand fill low spots of the trail. Familiar southwest desert plants—Mormon tea, four-wing saltbush, juniper and prickly-pear cactus—pepper the landscape. Cresting the final rise, I look down on a contrast of baking rust-brown sandstone disappearing into blue water. The ancient mudstone cracked, pieces of its story lie scattered about.

The inner wall of the right vertebral artery in my brainstem dissected thirty hours after I twisted my neck. It caused the shearing jolt that woke me. Fortunately, the outer wall retained its integrity and allowed the inner one to clot; otherwise I probably would have bled to death. Several blood clots released while mountain biking and lodged in my cerebellum, the control center for strength, balance and proprioception. The debilitating symptoms of my stroke took twenty-four hours to manifest. Months later Dr. Baten will tell me I used the textbook word *shearing* to describe the sudden headache caused by a vertebral artery dissection. It was the clue he needed to diagnose the origin of my stroke.

Shallow impressions of *Eubrontes* tracks are hard to see in the noon sunlight. I find one mid-way down the slope. Not a dinosaur genus, *Eubrontes* is the name given to these three-toed footprints, long middle toe pointing north, two shorter ones angled northwest and northeast from it. A sign on the slope says it is thought that the dinosaur that made these trackways was *Dilophosaurus*. A carnivorous biped, it was fifteen to twenty feet long, its hips four feet above the ground. Two hundred million years ago this landscape was sculpted like the Sahara Desert. Winds shaped sand dunes. Storms created oases called playas. *Dilophosaurus* fed at the playas and left footprints in wet sand. Seas crept over the land, fled away and returned, each one leaving its story in a layer of sediment. Stacked like pancakes, they compressed into rock. Forces deep in the Earth uplifted and tilted the red and tan cross-bedded layers. Now, erosive waters and wind in league with time patiently chip into their stories.

I follow a trackway, enjoying the prints' jazzy pace. Some tracks are shadows on rock. Others deep enough to hold rainfall. Was *Dilophosaurus* chasing prey? I think about the other-worldliness of large dinosaur footprints in the sparse Utah desert, and I wonder if they are any stranger than the mirage of Las Vegas. Stopping at a well-preserved footprint, I squat and place my hand beside it. It is twice as wide and long—at least eight inches by fifteen. *Eubrontes* means "true thunder." Sitting down, I cross my legs and meditate on a saying of Zen monk Tenkei, "Everyone has a natural essence that has no teacher. This is where you express yourself."

The first three days I was in the intensive care unit, my blood pressure spiked dangerously high. A monitor shrilled its alarm and the nurse assigned to me would immediately come into the dark room to check. Any spike could have resulted in a fatal dissection of the weakened artery. A second neurologist ran Doppler scans to ascertain the extent of blood flow through the artery and alluded to this scenario rather than stated it outright.

The extent of the stroke's damage was also a lurking worry. Often it takes days for deficits to manifest as neurons downstream from a clot slowly die due to lack of blood. Anxious questions were on everyone's unspoken mind: Will he be able to balance a checkbook? Slice a tomato? Would he walk? Drive? Grocery shop? But I was calm. I sensed I would ultimately thrive because everything *felt* right. Maybe it was the morphine.

Unable to swallow, I missed coffee. I maintained my sense of humor. On the fourth afternoon my parents were discussing lunch plans with a good friend of mine. Thinking I was sleeping, because that is what I mostly did, they whispered. I listened, then said, "Well folks, you know what this means. Dessert first from here on out." The dead having spoken, they quickly turned to face the bed, surprise on their faces. It was then they realized I would be ok.

Your hand alongside a dinosaur footprint, you wake from your privatized slumber and fully realize the existence of things long before you walked on the Earth's thin crust. Time holds space for life and living. Believing in their continuity through difficulties, you catch a glimpse of the teaching of Zen sage Dogen, "To know yourself is to forget yourself. To forget yourself is to become enlightened by all things." To become enlightened by things, I add, is to know yourself. Tawny rock sliding into aquamarine, the clear water at the reservoir's edge sends an invitation to swim. I accept.

A major challenge after my stroke was re-learning how to walk. Partly because of the nystagmus, I first had to master standing and balance. Encouragingly, my mother kept reminding me that as a toddler, I did not have this much trouble. In the physical rehabilitation unit of the hospital I made slow progress. My brain had to configure new neural pathways to accomplish things I never had to think about before. But eager to get on with it, I was enthusiastic and even had fun. Attentive to the angle of my hips over my knees and how my foot rocked on tile versus carpet, I was grateful for years of yoga practice. After two weeks I confidently walked out of the hospital aided by a four-prong cane.

At home in the Jemez Mountains I practiced walking on sidewalks for a week, then ventured to a nearby trail off the mesa top down into a canyon. Looking at the first twenty steep and rocky yards, I knew I would fall. I sat on my butt and inched down. Ecstatic I made it to the bottom, I stood and walked. On narrow sections, one edge falling away into the canyon, I leaned against the rock wall. I slid on my butt whenever I reached another tricky downhill. But I was on home ground, on earth. My dogs patiently waited for me. On the fourth day of walking the trail I did not have to resort to sliding.

Over the months and next few years, I increased the difficulty of my hiking excursions. Eventually I was backpacking in the Rocky Mountains and Grand Canyon again. None of my trips are easy for me. Residual effects from the stroke are heightened by terrain. I still have the nystagmus, and though greatly reduced, it is fatiguing and affects my balance. Uneven surfaces challenge my depth perception and I disorient easily. The left side of my body continually tingles. Most nights when I go to bed a burning begins in my left shoulder, travels down my arm and leg, and exits through fingers and toes. The intensity of the experience is a measure of my fatigue. My body's left side cannot sense hot or cold, a result Dr. Baten had no explanation for. But a positive is that I can swim in forbidden waters.

Torqued the right way, my vertebral artery dissected. Neither bad nor good, such things are natural, like the asteroid probably responsible for initiating the end of the dinosaur reign and subsequent rise of mammals. Hiking and backpacking in rugged alpine and canyon terrains, mammal me has learned to trust the tools and methods Nature uses to express her qualities. Meeting us in unexpected ways, they remind us of our vulnerability and resources. Once, while walking around a rock outcrop on a Grand Canyon trail, I surprised a four-foot rattlesnake slithering across it. She coiled and rattled her unique warning. *Her terrain.* I found another way around.

Such experiences follow us home. I suspect a pre-stroke wilderness adventure helped me find the right word in our large and diverse lexicon while being examined in the emergency room. Effortlessly, "shearing" rose from an unknown but re-remembered wildness, perhaps one kin to shorn treetops of a windblown forest.

Continually rising from bottomless depths, the world calls to say existence is a precious thing, one whose consequences we can't foresee. Part of the world, its student and disciple, I rise through the reservoir's waters not knowing what I will encounter at the surface. Perhaps the sky has clouded over or other dinosaur trackway seekers walk along the red cliffs where my clothes and hiking gear lie. My closed eyes sense a growing light. At the surface I see the sky remains cloudless and blue. The kayakers are gone. No other hikers scour the terrain. Revealing their secrets slowly, the prehistoric fossilized dunes beckon. The time has come to let the arid air reclaim the water cooling me, and then hike a different way back to the car.

MICHAEL G. SMITH is a chemist. His poetry has been published in *Borderlands: Texas Poetry Review, Cider Press Review, Nimrod,* the *Santa Fe Literary Review, Sin Fronteras, Superstition Review* and other journals and anthologies. The Oregon Poetry Association chose his poem "Disturbance Theory," which was based on hikes in old-growth and clear-cut forests, for its Fall 2017 New Poets Award. His books include *No Small Things* (Tres Chicas Books, 2014), *The Dippers Do Their Part,* a collaboration with Laura Young of haibun and katagami from their Shotpouch Cabin residency (Miriam's Well, 2015), and *Flip Flop,* a collection of haiku co-written with Miriam Sagan (Miriam's Well, 2017).

Common Mom

by Jennifer D. Munro

"I heard there's a Great Egret down at the harbor!" I told my thirteen-year-old. Finally, a bird so distinctive I stood a chance of not only seeing but identifying it. Hard to miss an albino duck the size of a barstool.

"You've seen one before." Ben glanced up from his birding field guide. Friendless, he has memorized them the way I scrutinized *Tiger Beat* at his age.

"I have?"

"In California with Grandma. You wrote the date and place in your bird book."

"I did? What book?"

"The small red square one."

This is a boy who can't remember to turn off the lights or cap the toothpaste. He can detect and name a flitting, tan, thumb-sized bird in dense foliage, yet doesn't notice he's emptied half the recycling outside the bin.

Ben returned to his book. "I've seen egrets on vacation."

"But they're not seen *here*."

"The Great Egret is common, Mom."

Moms were all too common for Ben. I'm his twelfth. He had migrated through foster care until my husband and I adopted him at age nine. Ben was shoved from too many nests, too soon, too often.

The next time we talked birds. Ben was excited. I heard him say, "I heard there's a red pole at Green Lake!"

"For a special flag?"

"No!" He thrust an open guidebook at me. "A Common Redpoll!"

"Ah. Well, if they're common, why the excitement?"

"They're not common *here*! They're a rare winter visitor!"

I studied the picture. "Why not call it Uncommon Red Beret, then?" My incompetence boosts his confidence; often it's not a stretch for me to feign ignorance.

He rolled his eyes. "There's Common Merganser, Common Goldeneye, Common Eider...but there's no bird called Uncommon, Mom."

When Ben first came to our family, we had nothing in common, not even a shared past.

I first took up birding as a peaceful escape from my troubled son—we'd had difficulty bonding. But I could barely pick out my preferred mustard on a crowded grocery store shelf, much less track and identify chirping blurs in the treetops; it still took me a while to spot my own son in a classroom. The birding guides, with descriptions like "feathering extends far down upper mandible," were as incomprehensible to me as what I'd read in Ben's social services case history that filled an IBM box.

Unexpectedly, Ben hijacked my solitary respite. Rather than communing with nature by myself, I ended up chauffeuring him at dawn to fragrant sewage treatment ponds, the all-you-can-eat buffets for waterfowl. Once we're there, he often heaves out sighs at my dimwittedness, a longsuffering prodigy saddled with an inept tutor, but he likes being the guide. Too often in life he has been the confused one trailing behind.

On one of those early mornings, a self-proclaimed bird photographer with a two-foot lens trailed us around the pond. We shadowed a cluster of birds he hadn't seen scratching in the frost.

"He couldn't identify Golden-crowned Sparrows!" I said to Ben afterward, sharing a moment of connection with our mutual superiority. "They're so common!"

"They're not technically common," he corrected.

"But even *I* can recognize them!"

"True." He saw my point, possibly a first.

He darted ahead while I dawdled at a pair of ducks with spectacular hairdos. I dubbed them Phyllis Diller and *Young Frankenstein's* Madeline Kahn.

A David Bowie bird, big as a platform boot, flaunted its glam makeup on a high wire nearby. Attempting an arty photo, I looked directly up at the bird's "undertail," the term on my guide's anatomical diagram.

Ben trotted back to me. "Mom, you missed seeing a Common Loon! *Again.*"

Targeted squarely beneath the next dropping turd, I tarried—an ordinary double-chinned loon.

Ben tugged me out of excrement's way. "You're weird, Mom."

Not really. Flightless, certainly—his first mom who's not taking off. But, doing what it takes to help her unusual fledgling soar, just another Common Mom.

JENNIFER D. MUNRO's work has appeared in numerous journals and anthologies, including *Salon, Gulf Coast, North American Review, Massachusetts Review, Full Grown People,* and *Zyzzyva.* Munro's blog, StraightNoChaserMom.com, won First Place in the 2015 National Society of Newspaper Columnists contest (under 100k monthly visitors category), and her work was a Top Ten Finalist in the Erma Bombeck Humor Writing Competition.

A Walk to Divide Meadow

by Nicola Waldron

We pull on our trusty, sand-encrusted boots, stuff Clif bars in our fanny packs, and head out to Point Reyes, one of my favorite places on this far western edge of the continent that I've come, hesitatingly, to call home. It's been a long journey, first across the wide ocean from England, where I was born and lived till I was thirty—stuck, impatient—then New England (exiled, married, slightly shaken), and finally out west to California and into the tectonic state of infertility. This costly revelation has catapulted my husband, Jim, and I into a rutted moonscape. Dark and featureless save for its trip-you-up craters, the land trembles and falls away, wholly unpredictable under our once so certain, youthful feet.

It's Easter weekend, glorious, fresh. The April sun filters through layers of coastal fog that shift to reveal, then veil again, the rounded guardian peaks in whose shadows we live. Ahead of me stretches spring break: a holy week I will observe in my own new-fangled way, not in any church, but here in our little cabin in the Marin woods beside a raging spring-fed creek, my hand pressed over sanctified belly.

Yesterday, Good Friday—so marked on the calendar at the Catholic school where I teach poetry to eager girls—I lay on a surgical bed dressed in a hospital smock and a coronet of rosebuds, praying in my own non-specific, post-millennial way while a Jewish doctor peered with great solemnity up my vagina. He suctioned fifteen drug-induced eggs from my ovaries through the equivalent of an overlong drinking straw, then handed them to a cheery embryologist who dropped them, ever so gently, into a hospitable pool of growth medium, along with a phial of my husband's hopeful, abashed sperm—all this on the far side of the Golden Gate Bridge, across whose dizzying span I've passed, face pressed hard, wonderingly, up inside the windscreen.

Now, in the company of my bewildered spouse, I head north and west, away from the lab, to a gentle, grassy field called Divide Meadow out at the Point Reyes National Seashore. The Point sits on the rift between two peculiarly discrete biospheres, the serendipitous result of an intriguing natural history. It's a nomadic landmass that has drifted over three hundred miles from her mountain home to arrive, beautiful visitor, at her current lush residence in the north. The guidebooks call this temperate headland "displaced" or "suspect" terrain; it seems there's no escaping the notion that foreign implants are untrustworthy and unwelcome, no matter how they might enrich the landscape. (As the wife of a restoration ecologist, I have done my own share, brow furrowed, of ripping out stubborn 'invasives' like the pretty, feathered tamarind.)

Point Reyes, which lies right on the San Andreas Fault, is a place of historic tremor, potentially great danger, and, paradoxically, of utter calm. The short path that leads from the Bear Valley Visitor Center—a spectacularly repurposed cow barn—is called the Earthquake Trail, a reminder to those who venture here that there is little to be gained from avoiding perilous truths: we are but motes floating in nature's brilliance. Jim and I glance that way before striding resolutely in the direction of the broad, reliable track we almost always choose.

I am anxious to cover distance and get my blood pumping. This will be my last opportunity to exercise for at least a week, since after the implantation in my uterus of any successfully growing embryos on Sunday (also Passover as it happens—I fret about the doctor's obligations), I've been instructed to lie down and "think positive thoughts." I've already set up my pillows, books, tapes, and teacups; an altar, complete with "magic" eggs of fogged glass that glow a soft gold when I lift them to the light. If pregnancy results, I speculate, this hike may be the last one I'll get to enjoy for some time. I've begun my final round of shots—progesterone, the sustainer, the hormonal elixir that will cozy-up my uterus and put me in a state of expectancy. I have been expectant for so long now.

I feel oddly empty, my ovaries an echoing, abandoned sanctuary. I've been nurturing those growing eggs like a brooding hen, and now they've been vacuumed out of me. Across the bridge in the city of St. Francis, the kindly fosterer, cells are dividing and amassing in their heady soup; not migrating down the coral strait intended by nature, but cultivated instead by a scientist, the embryologist I barely met in my giggly pre-operative swoon. The only thing to do—the right thing, it seems—is to go out in nature and take a very long walk, to make on behalf of our little, distant morula the kind of arduous and lovely journey it—*he? she?*—has been denied.

We pass the trailhead with a kind of bionic vigor. Hand-in-hand, step matching step, we strike out beneath the grand shade of Douglas firs and Bishop pines that line the path. Always quiet in spite of its popularity, this first part of the trail boasts few dramatic surprises: just two graceful, restorative miles that focus the senses on what grows and moves on either side of the wide, straight path. The eye begins at the luminous intensity of infant ferns and oxalis at ground level, then travels up past sweetly hued snapdragons to the steep banks of towering conifers that shelter the passer-by from all but the most ferocious of suns. When a deer or the occasional bobcat bounds from the brush, the watcher's lucky heart leaps with the unrestrained thrill of sharing the world with these creatures. Here is a place where life goes about its business of reproduction and survival, paying little heed to the humans that tramp by with their spotting scopes. Here is nature, pure and wild and good, inhabited by a stunning diversity of creatures and the humans most likely to love them—the naturalist, the creative mind, the soul in search of universal communion. The hopeful. The earth kept safe from maverick building contractors.

We are accompanied almost all the way by a pristine, spirited creek that continues its infinite journey even while we are elsewhere mired in very human, temporal questions—should we, and what if, and why not—that come with the attempt at IVF. The creek acts as a sage, a cleansing force, and as we meander beside it, stopping every now and then to name a bird or tree or flower, I become further convinced that there is no way that this strangely artificial and futuristic gambit in which Jim and I have been engaged might not pay off. Signs of fertility flourish all around us—waters gush over damp earth, the sun gleams down in celestial shafts, colors pop up wherever you look, and everywhere, that particular vibrant springtime greenness that cracks open winter.

The trail ends six miles on at the edge of the continent with a grand view of the Pacific. We've seen the ocean crash and recede through the fabulous arching rock formations; the pelicans swoop and rise, buffeted aloft on thermal currents. Today, however, we stop well before those cliffs. We have had enough of the perilous edge.

We come to rest exactly halfway along the trail to the precipice, 300 feet above sea level. At the crest of a thigh-burning hill, we turn a corner and there it is spread out before us, practically insisting we sit among its tall grasses and majestic trees: Divide Meadow. Some hardy crew has even provided a set of great fallen logs, carved to function as couches.

We walk, as we always do, to the seat farthest from the path, which offers a feeling of open communion with its neighbors while retaining a sense of innate privacy. This is a place where we can talk about the greatest of challenges or conflicts, and the spirit of the place imperceptibly helps us to resolution.

It is always hard to get up and continue the long hike to the sea, or to return to the trailhead after sitting here; I feel I should remain, wait for the moon to come up, and sleep there under her cool light. It is that rare place in which nature feels utterly benign, and even the night animals seem harmless. Once, we glimpsed a group of white fallow deer, a family of misplaced exotics that appeared mystically as if out of some Narnian dream. Alas, the National Parks Service destroyed these gracious animals in a program of "exotics eradication." For the "exotic," or immigrant like me—Darwinian misfit, too—the irony, and the sense of threat, is not lost.

Jim and I lean against one another, sharing sips of water, looking out at this gentle landscape. We are already taking care of my body, not overdoing it, though there is no real physical reason for this caution. Time passes, and we lose ourselves in the ether, as raptors and seabirds ride the breeze, and people—who seem, for once, as innocuous as the terrain—come and go. We don't speak; the words seem to have been sucked from us. When I hold out my hands, Jim pulls me up and we amble to the car in a state balanced somewhere between acceptance and quiet resolve.

Back at the cabin, we fall together on the bed, tired in the best way, and, though—or perhaps because—that night is wrapped in sanctity, we make love without expectation or consideration of consequence. We have been to the divide. There, we sat looking out over the shimmering landscape towards the inscrutable vanishing point of our future, expecting nothing but that we might rest awhile and breathe. We took refuge at the median between threshold and destination. The mythic deer did not appear, but we knew they were out there feasting somewhere on new spring growth. Their absence reminded us that it is the mystery of things that matters. If we are meant to receive a child, we will bring that baby to the meadow and sit on that same bench under the big trees, in the protective shade. And if we are to remain two, we will go there still. We'll hike, then, all the way to the sea.

NICOLA WALDRON, a native of England, is a graduate of Cambridge University and the Bennington College Writing Seminars. The recipient of the United Kingdom's Bridport Poetry Prize and, most recently, *Jasper* magazine's Broad River Prize for prose (2014), her work has recently been featured in *Agni, Sonora Review, The Common, Mom Egg Review* and others. Her poetry chapbook, *Girl at the Watershed*, was published in 2013 by Stepping Stones Press. She teaches creative writing at the University of South Carolina.

Loving Stones

by Kathleen Hayes Phillips

What's in this bag? Rocks? It is barely daylight. I am leaving Ireland. The man carrying my suitcase to the car speaks in that soft Irish way, but he is not kidding. I shrug my shoulders. We both laugh at the strange behavior of tourists, their souvenirs. I don't tell him the truth. My bag *is* full of rocks. I call them stones. I always come home from a trip carrying stones.

The obsession started when I was ten years old. My parents are to blame. It was my father who took me to Pebble Beach in Door County. He found the spot in the 1920s when he was a young man working a summer job picking cherries in what is called The Thumb of Wisconsin. In his 40s, he enjoyed taking his family to the sights he'd discovered as a young adult. This is where he learned to skip stones across the water of Eagle Harbor. He wanted to teach his son and daughter the joys of that ancient skill.

My brother learned. I did not. My stones always landed with a plunk in the shallow water two inches from my bare toes. That is when mother took over. To soothe my pout, she helped me find flat, smooth stones to take home. By the end of the walk, my hands and pockets were full. And that was the beginning.

In adulthood, the obsession lay dormant until my husband and I went to Ireland for our 25th wedding anniversary. It was early morning, in the town of Kenmare, not far from Cork. We needed to walk off our full Irish breakfast, so wandered further into the town. There, just beyond the post office, before the town was awake, I saw it ... not a beach with smooth, pocket-sized pebbles, but a circle of raw granite boulders. There were no tourists in sight ... just us and a ring of stones set in browned grass in the center of the town. It was so quiet, church quiet. I could almost touch the silence. I wanted to blurt out ... *Who, what, why, and how* ... but did not, just walked into and around this mysterious place. Something special was remembered here or learned or wondered about. I had to find out more.

We found the tourist center and bought a booklet explaining what we had seen. Maps showed the location of stone circles like the one we'd seen—and also ring forts and cairns and standing stones. The area was filled with wonder.

My husband and I adopted a new itinerary: no straight routes anywhere. Maps we carried were rich with a new vocabulary, a language of the distant past, heavy with mystery and history. We climbed stiles and wandered in sheep pastures, wending our way through bog lands and farmers' fields. *Why?* To find more about these monuments to time and the people who, thousands of years ago, not only held and carried, but honored stones.

The interest continued when we got home. I found a mother-lode of information in Scott Peck's book, *In Search of Stones*. It not only explained my past collecting, but my new enthusiasm. Our trips changed into searches, morphed into pilgrimages. Jim's eyes stayed on the road ahead while I watched to see what was passing on either side. Every field and hillside, every farmyard and two-lane country road held the possibility for adventure. Once, I pulled at his arm, getting an immediate reaction, of course. We parked the car and climbed over a stile, finding there, in the middle of a field, a perfect ring of stones.

I was not satisfied with stones in my pocket. I wanted to know them better than that. I wanted to find them, touch their rough or smooth surfaces, walk among them, lean against them. I had so many questions to ask and loved the search for answers.

In Arizona, we found petroglyphs on the cliffs along a golf course, combined the dances of Lughnassah in Brittany with visits to passage graves, Orkney fiddle sessions with a moonlight walk to the ring of Brodgar. We saw stones piled along the road in New Zealand and on the beaches of Door County in Wisconsin.

Our vocabulary grew. So did our searches. We planned our routes around cairns, dolmans and wedge tombs where the living piled stones to speak about the dead. And less publicized places where stones were planted in the ground: monoliths, steles and ogham stones reaching up to link earth with the sky. Other humans wrenched these stones from the ground and arranged them to mark the passage of time or the seasons of the year, the movements of the moon or sun ... or human life.

The stones told stories of those who honored our connection to the earth, ancestors who wondered about what was beyond the flow of daily living here in this place—beyond the dawn and sunset, the changing seasons, this life we enter and leave. We listened and looked at life differently, continuing to follow the stones until we were no longer able to travel.

But we never forgot the wonder we felt for the first time in Ireland. Jim decided he wanted his ashes scattered there. We were not ready then for more than a gentle touch on that possibility and headed back to more solid ground. We talked of our younger selves, full of wonder and finding places known only to the two of us. Sacred places, we called them, full of awe. I never forgot those conversations.

When Jim died at 86, my family knew I would take his ashes to Ireland. After the services were over and life started up again with a new and unfamiliar pattern, Jim took over, planning my journey from afar. All I did was google once and then follow his directions.

I typed in WEST COAST RETREATS. Taos appeared, Santa Fe and Seattle. Then the search took a leap to the southwest of Ireland to a place named Anam Cara on the Beara Peninsula. *Anam cara* means *soul friend* in Gaelic. The words were familiar to me for I had once read a book of the same name by John O'Donaighue, an Irish poet and philosopher. And I had chosen readings from his *Anam Cara* for Jim's funeral service. It seemed an intriguing coincidence. I was not surprised to find that yes, here was a writers' workshop in September. Yes, it was for poets, and yes, there was an opening. The workshop would start on Jim's birthday. How much more did I need?

The Beara Peninsula is in County Cork, near Dingle and the Ring of Kerry, one of the fingers of land sticking into the ocean at the bottom of any map of Ireland. I could picture the area. Jim and I tiptoed along its edge, but never explored Beara itself. I liked the idea of traveling to an area not filled with memories of us together.

The trip was without incident. I landed safely and was soon driving with break-neck speed along one narrow hedge-lined road after another. I saw a sign for Kenmare. In a flash it was gone, leaving only the memories. From that point on, nothing looked familiar. The drive took four hours, but it seemed in no time at all I was settled in a rambling stone house set on a hillside overlooking Cloulagh Bay.

The workshop provided time to write and share the process with six other poets. We worked and ate together in the mornings. Afternoons allowed us free time. We walked the narrow roads lined with blackberry hedges that led to the town of Eyeries, its main street lined with rainbow houses. There, we talked to a wise-woman. We watched storms move across the mountains and sipped milky tea at all hours of the day and night.

Three of my fellow-writers were Irish. One day, after writing all morning, one in the group offered to drive us to the end of the peninsula. It was raining. The small car fought the gusty wind. Patches of fog settled on the heath and moved across the narrow road. We were close to the edge of the cliff, the sea dashing its waves on rock-strewn shores below.

Wind and fog blurred the car windows, and the narrow, winding road made it impossible to stop. I watched silently from the back seat when … there, in the middle of a rain-swept field, I saw a wedge tomb, its familiar triangular shape rising out of the mist. I did not say a word, just marked its place on the foggy window … *right there.*

If Jim had been driving I would have grabbed his arm, eliciting an immediate response and, despite the weather, we would have stopped. I know we would have stopped. He always did. He might have laughed at my love of stones, but he always stopped and climbed the stile or held the wire, plodding ahead of me across sheep pastures, and empty moors, warning me where *not* to step. We would have examined the tomb as if it was the first we saw, commenting on the size, the impossible location and splendor of the setting, the miracle of people dragging such stones to this place amid rugged mountains and stone cliffs falling away into tumultuous seas. Here they buried their dead. Here was their place for memory. Remembering was why I came.

Those same poets who wrote and walked with me, knew why I came and helped me find the Kealinche River running alongside and beyond Anam Cara. One of them, a younger and more intrepid climber, explored its banks. One day, equipped with borrowed wellies and a stout walking stick, she led me down twisting stairs through a green world not unlike a rain forest. I held tight to a guide-line, watching my every step and trusting her to find the way. Safe at the bottom, we walked along the river. The quiet Kealinche changed. When out of sight, the river took its own downward path, becoming rapids. The rushing water, forged its own way over and around boulders left here by some ancient upheaval, then calmed as it ran under a wooden bridge, making its way to the estuary and the sea beyond.

This is where I scattered Jim's ashes, not alone accompanied by memories and words written by my family, but with my *anam cara*, the soul friends I found in this place. Together we walked down the stairs, stood to watch the powerful cascade before us and then moved to the wooden bridge. His ashes floated in the air for a moment and came to rest on the brown waters below us. We watched as they flowed out of sight.

The next morning, I walked to the estuary where the Kealinche met the sea, a place of sand and stone where sea birds circle overhead and gather along the shores, wading and feeding in the brackish waters. The tide was out, so I wandered along the shoreline, watching rivulets move toward the sea. I filled my pockets with stones, each telling the layered story of how it came to be, some scarred by their shattering, others smoothed by sand and waves. They would be added to stones brought home from other journeys … those piled in a birdbath on my small porch, displayed in bowls and baskets in my apartment, and on the desk where I write, kept in sight to remind me of my own path to wonder. They hold the stories of this place and time, helping me to tell my own story, how I began this journey without Jim beside me, but found he was with me all the way, such memories never heavy at all.

KATHLEEN HAYES PHILLIPS is 82, and lives in a senior residence in Milwaukee, Wisconsin. She taught for many years, and began writing 20 years ago. Much of her inspiration comes from her travels with her husband over the years. She finds the muse in the city as well as the country, is a member of the Wisconsin Fellowship of Poets, and her work has appeared in many publications and anthologies.

Going Solo

by Kathleen Canrinus

"The mountains are calling, and I must go," I say to my husband Don, borrowing the words John Muir spoke to his spouse when he set out for the Sierra. It is mid-September, the end of the hiking season in the high mountains. Don has given up asking questions about the details of my trips. He knows there are none. No, I don't know whether I'll backpack. I don't know exactly where I'll hike or even where I'll stay at Tuolumne Meadows. I just know that I must go.

Don is a planner and an organizer. He's very good at it. I have organizational ability. I can and do plan yet sometimes prefer spontaneity and leaving a few things to chance. He'd be willing to admit that plans can take you only so far and cannot guarantee a great or even good time. I say that leaving arrangements turns a trip into an adventure—up to a point.

Taking off without reservations or an itinerary means packing for every contingency—car camping, a High Sierra Camp, backpacking. Worst case, I pitch my tent at the walk-in campground for backpackers. It doesn't take long to pack. I have already used the backpack gear this summer on a week-long trip with my twenty-five-year-old daughter, and Don and I have just returned from an annual three-family camping trip at the beach, always a bit of an ordeal for him. He is not a camper.

I know that Don wishes I wouldn't go. He worries, and he does not understand my desire to go. He suffers through the annual beach camping trip for my sake but doesn't really get why anyone would choose to be uncomfortable.

"Everything is harder," he argues as if logic applies. "Making a cup of coffee is a ten-step process. And it's a five-minute walk to bathrooms that don't have electricity or hot water."

Naturally, I want my husband to love what I love.

"But don't you find the scenery stunning? Don't you enjoy living outdoors, simply, without a lot of stuff?"

As if to put to rest once and for all the conversations in which I attempt to convince him of the wonders of camping in the mountains, he recently revealed that when he was young, his family had never even owned a tent.

Don is a beach person. He grew up body surfing on Southern California beaches and still enjoys a swim in the ocean followed by a long nap on hot sand.

"My idea of camping is the Ahwahnee," he tells me.

I inherited my mother's love of the mountains and camping. I don't mind that everything's harder. I don't mind inconvenience. I don't mind that the day begins with wiggling out of a warm, cozy sleeping bag and layering up in preparation for hiking in the chill air to the bathroom. I don't mind the many steps to morning coffee. They slow me down, one of the reasons I go to the mountains. Making a cup of coffee can start with fetching water and always includes rooting about in a bear box or canister, using fingers numb with cold to tinker with an often temperamental stove, and balancing self and objects on uneven surfaces. The long process contributes to my enjoyment of the result. I attend to each step with care. While I am doing my coffee-making meditation—always with Peet's French Roast—I take in the view from the "kitchen window." When my Sierra cup is full, I carry it to a flat rock near a stream or lake. From there, I sit and watch the light travel from peak to valley, down the granite faces of cliffs as the sun rises. I let the pine needle that lands in my coffee remain there. So, unlike the twelve-track life at home, it's a one-track life in the mountains, made up of tiny achievements.

When the car is packed, and I am ready to leave for the mountains, Don walks me out.

"Don't do anything dumb," he says, resigned to my folly.

"I am always careful," I reply.

Don gives me a look. We both know all too well that accidents happen. I once broke my leg on a familiar trail one mile from home and a quarter mile from work during my lunch hour.

"I'll stay on the main trails," I assure him, while silently acknowledging that slipping and falling is likely when hiking forty miles of steep rocky trails. Despite the experience in my own neighborhood, falls rarely result in serious injury, I tell myself.

Not one who seeks solitude, Don turns toward the house to begin his solo week. He is a photographer, and while I'm away, he'll work on his projects. As I back the car out of the driveway, I visualize the first views of the magnificent granite masses that characterize the Tuolumne Meadows region and the enormous flat meadows themselves.

During the five-hour drive, I listen to Stanford neuroscientist Robert Sapolsky's eight-part lecture on Biology and Human Behavior: The Neurological Origins of Individuality. From these fascinating talks, I begin to understand how biology at the cellular level affects human behavior. I am forced to consider that I'm off to the mountains—and Don isn't—not because I am an individual in control of my life but as a result of my brain chemistry. Not everyone, I extrapolate from the talks, has pleasure pathways that can be stimulated by the words "exfoliating granite."

Thanks to Dr. Sapolsky, the drive passes quickly. Luck is with me, and by late afternoon, I am settled in a campsite at the Tuolumne Meadows Campground. After pitching the tent and setting up a simple kitchen, I spend an hour walking by the river, soaking up its sound and energy while inhaling deep breaths of thin, pine-scented air. When I discover a secluded swimming hole, I leave my clothes on a rock and ease myself into the chilly water, but just up to my chin.

Before the light fades, I return to camp, eat dinner, and secure the food. Sunset marks the end of an alpine day, just as sunrise marks the beginning. It's still light when I crawl into my tent. Possible hiking destinations flood my mind, but there's no need to plan yet. I decide to wait until after breakfast to choose a trail and instead snuggle down into my sleeping bag to rest if not to sleep. As my eyes close, I welcome like old friends the familiar twin feelings specific to the high mountains at nightfall—a primitive fear of the dark night ahead paired with longing for the return of the light. I know that trust in the likelihood of surviving the night will eventually override both.

By the time I leave for home days later, I have taken four long hikes, three to favorite destinations and one to a new spot, Clouds Rest. The last was a corker, fourteen miles in a day. It included slipping and skidding down a rock, a fall that left me with skinned elbows. I decide not to mention it at home. No need to mention that I came very close to requiring a headlamp to complete the hike. I also won't tell Don that I strayed off the trail in the Ten Lakes Basin and did a bit of cross-country hiking (nothing dangerous).

I love many things about the high mountains, but most of all, I love the rock. There is something in me that responds to the ancient, unchanging formations: Mount Conness, Lembert Dome, the Grand Canyon of the Tuolumne, Cathedral, Shepherd's and Unicorn Peaks. The granite in all its permutations never fails to remind me of my place in the universe. I am small, and I am comforted by that knowledge.

That life flourishes in such extreme conditions also comforts me. The plants, trees, and animals of the High Sierra remind me that maybe I too can survive the human equivalent of an Ice Age or bitter cold winter or short growing season.

I feel satisfied with my solo trip. I have spent five days not thinking about much more than where to place my feet and poles and where to eat lunch—days when mind was still, and my body moved. With a promise to return next summer, I say goodbye to the mountains.

From somewhere near Modesto, I call Don. There's relief in his voice as he welcomes me back to civilization. He won't need to call Search and Rescue—not this time anyway. He'll have dinner ready, he says.

The eighth lecture is just ending as I pull into the driveway. I stay in the car to listen as Dr. Sapolsky finishes reviewing the potential differences among humans at the cellular level, brain to brain, the explanation for our uniqueness. I accept that the relationship of neurotransmitters to receptors at certain synapses in my brain may have something to do with why I am a mountain person, and Don is not. Since I am sixty-four, I accept also that one day, the biology of aging will end solo hiking trips to the high mountains. I reach across the seat for my daypack; I feel grateful for the gift of a few summer days in the Sierra and resolve that for now and for as long as I am able, when the mountains call, I will go.

KATHLEEN CANRINUS has been writing stories from her life since she retired from teaching elementary school. She lives in Palo Alto, California, with her husband.

#hatchwatch2016

by Patti Jeane Pangborn

It's morning but still dark outside, and the moon is a sliver. A few cars can be heard on the nearby road, but otherwise all is still and quiet. A shrill cry pierces the night air, and I can just make out the silhouette of a bald eagle in the darkness. Harriet is where she has been all night, incubating her two eggs high up in her nest in a slash pine tree. Harriet is vocalizing to her mate, M15, probably telling him it's his turn to sit on the eggs or asking him to go get her a fish for breakfast. M15 moves on a nearby branch, revealing himself in the darkness. He looks down at Harriet and seems to contemplate his next move. I watch them trade off egg incubation duty, eat a fish that M15 brings to the nest, and aerate the nest material all while the sun comes up. I'm drinking my first cup of coffee, checking my email and Facebook. I close my laptop and the eagles disappear, but I'm comforted by the fact that I can check on them again later.

The live feed that I was watching and have continued to watch obsessively since December 27, 2016 was streaming from "Camera 1" of the Southwest Florida Eagle Cam (SWFEC) starring Harriet and

M15, a mated pair of bald eagles in North Fort Myers, Florida.[1] Harriet was roosting two eggs that were due to hatch any day. I'd found out about this eagle cam on Facebook. Local news channels and several of my Facebook friends started sharing the live feed around Christmas time, and I found myself watching at least once a day. My growing affection for these creatures was not unexpected.

I grew up in the middle of nowhere in Michigan. In fact, my hometown isn't even big enough to be considered a town. We've got one blinking red light at the only intersection in "downtown" Stanwood, which consists of a single street where you can visit the bank, eat at the Corner Café, and buy some feed for your livestock at Feed N' Seed. The village of Stanwood is full of Amish people, farmers, and woods. I played in the woods often as a child and I was always interested in the local wildlife.

I remember the summer a pair of killdeer built their nest in our yard. I would check on the eggs every day, driving the poor birds nuts as one pretended to be hurt to draw me away from the nest and the other guarded the eggs bravely against my potentially egg-crushing feet. Eventually, the eggs hatched, and the fuzzy baby birds were all I could think about. I wanted to hold them, but knew I couldn't. I used to stare at them longingly from the kitchen window. One of the eggs never hatched and once the birds left the nest for the season, my mother took the egg and cracked it open to show me what was inside. The half-formed body of a baby bird revealed itself, slimy in the egg. I remember a mixture of fascination and devastation, as I recalled the adult birds patiently sitting on this egg even after the other eggs in the nest had hatched.

As an adult, my mother and I still bond over bird talk. She put up bird feeders in the yard and I bought her a book called *Birds of Michigan*. She texts me often to tell me things like the pileated woodpecker is back on the light pole or the hummingbirds are fighting over the feeder.

I remember when my third-grade teacher read Dr. Dolittle books to my class during reading time. I wanted so badly to be able to talk

---

1. "Live Eagle Cam," *Southwest Florida Eagle Cam - Main View*, accessed March 3, 2017, http://www.dickpritchettrealestate.com/eagle-feed.html.

to animals after hearing those stories. I'd go home and try to communicate with my cat, Odie. If he held my gaze for any length of time, I was convinced he could understand me. I wanted to be able to communicate with any animal I encountered and still do, but the difficulty is in the encounter itself. Most animals I've watched or interacted with have been house pets or in captivity. What was most amazing about watching Harriet and M15 on the nest was that these eagles were not in captivity and this wasn't a previously filmed event, prepped for human viewing. These were wild birds, and people all over the world could watch them and talk about them without disturbing the nest, in real time. Somehow, that feeling that I am participating in the exploitation of animals that happens when I go to the zoo, waiting for them to do something interesting in their tiny, fake habitats was not present here.

When I lived in Chicago, I went to the Lincoln Park Zoo several times, mostly because it was free admission but also because it boasts "naturalistic exhibits" and "awe-inspiring animal encounters." Most of the exhibits have an open-air section that allows the animals to be outside or inside, and visitors can view them from both areas. During one visit, the jaguar was standing in his outdoor habitat, roaring and growling repeatedly. Zoo-goers, including myself, were thrilled. It was easy to imagine that he was showing off for us or saying hello.

Later, on another visit, I saw the same jaguar, but this time he was pacing his indoor enclosure. He kept walking back and forth in front of the glass, turning at exactly the same spot over and over again. A large cardboard box had been placed in his enclosure to give him something to play with. It looked like it had been gnawed on. I remember feeling a sense of disappointment that the animal wasn't outside, roaring for me again. Watching the wild eagles online allowed for guilt-free viewing. I could watch, comfortable in the fact that the creatures were not caged or limited in any way by my viewing. The sacrifice that came with this guilt-free viewing was that they would never know I was watching. I could never hope to catch their eye and imagine they might notice and think about me.

Observing the eagles, who were carefully watching over their eggs, made me want to protect them. I wanted them to know I was watching, to reciprocate the feelings I was having. I wanted to meet them, pet them, feed them bites of raw fish. But these birds didn't need me. They don't know I exist and never will. This part of the watching felt sad and a bit unfair. Here I am, hungrily tuning in every chance I get to satisfy my urge to watch, and make them part of my life. But what are they getting in return? If they could, would they give permission for this intrusion?

Thousands of viewers tune in daily to watch these eagles. Most of the time, the eagles are doing absolutely nothing. While incubating her eggs, Harriet would fall asleep out of pure boredom, but the view counter claimed ten thousand people were tuned in. Unlike a wildlife program on public television, edited for maximum excitement, the eagles' daily lives were incredibly uneventful. But what was most exciting about the experience was the ability to tune in at any time, from just about anywhere with a decent cell signal or Wi-Fi, and know the cams would be streaming and others would be tuned in as well.

The SWFEC website, run by the Pritchett family, says that the best place to view the nest is from your desktop at home, where you can switch from three different camera angles. Camera 1 is tied to the nest tree approximately six feet above the nest and features an infrared light to provide night-time viewing of the sleeping eagles. Camera 2 is about 60 feet away from the nest, strapped to another tree. Camera 3 is positioned near the pond on the property and serves as a way for viewers to catch Harriet and M15 in the act of bathing. [2] All of the cameras are capable of picking up sound, and longtime viewers have learned to tell the difference between Harriet's and M15's calls. Viewers have the Pritchetts to thank for this 24/7 all access pass to an eagle pair's daily nesting life.

My obsession with the eagles grew beyond the eagles themselves. I was fascinated by the Pritchett family who seemed to

---

2. Information gathered from "Fast Facts" on the SWFEC website. "Live Eagle Cam," *Southwest Florida Eagle Cam - Main View*, accessed March 3, 2017, http://www.dickpritchettrealestate.com/eagle-feed.html.

be running the SWFEC website while also running a real estate business, and had the technological know-how to set up these high-powered web cams. Part of me wondered if they were profiting off the eagles in some way. I decided to email their info account to see if someone might be willing to provide me with more information, and was pleasantly surprised when Ginnie Pritchett McSpadden enthusiastically responded, offering to personally answer any questions I had. I admit, I immediately Googled her, expecting an elderly retiree who probably had nothing to do with the actual website or cams, but who was in charge of responding to all the silly emails from fans. Instead, via Facebook stalking, I quickly discovered that Ginnie is a professional woman, probably in her 30s, and seems just as obsessed with the eagles as I am. Her Facebook feed is full of shared video and images from the SWFEC website, but not in a self-promoting sort of way. Once, she shared a video from BuzzFeed News of the eagles on their nest on her timeline, with the words, "Someone pinch me!" She seems to be in awe of the popularity of the cams.

"The eagles have been a part of our farm since 2007," Ginnie wrote in her email response to my inquiry about the horses that are sometimes seen grazing in view of the cameras. She also wrote about how the property has been in their family for over 85 years and was originally a vacation home for her grandfather, Richard (Dick) Pritchett. "The farm today is home to a horse stable and various activities that are operated by members of our extended family," she responded. Ginnie, along with her brother Andy and her husband Dave are the most involved with the operation and set-up of the cameras and SWFEC website. The live streaming of the SWFEC started in the 2012-2013 nesting season, which, in Florida, is between October 1 and May 15. Between the three of them and 15 devoted volunteers, they keep watch on the nest during nesting season almost constantly. They are able to remotely operate the cameras, often zooming in to focus on the smallest details, like feathers growing in on that season's new eaglet or a fish spine left over from lunch. The invisible hands behind the cameras have affectionately been nicknamed "Zoomies" by regular viewers.

I had imagined some sort of special equipment set up in a secret bunker, with knobs and buttons to operate the eagle cams. In reality, it's much less high-tech. "The setup is actually just one computer and can be controlled remotely by multiple users," Ginnie explained in her email. "It was a lot of trial and error in the beginning, a lot of late nights, and trips to the cams to restart them. But now in Season 5 we have a system down and each season we strive to do better." The SWFEC has been broadcasting the adventures of this eagle family every year since the 2012-2013 season, gaining thousands of viewers each year. The Pritchett family does not profit from the website or the eagles.

The goal to provide information to viewers on a more personal level prompted the Pritchetts to add a chat feature to the SWFEC website. Ginnie wrote, "We didn't know about chat when we first started the cams actually and after multiple requests for one, we finally got it together and that is when our volunteer team really came together. We also realized that this was another great step to connect the dots on education and learning while watching. We hope that through participating or simply reading chat, viewers will learn something about the eagles and take that with them and hopefully respect the eagles even more and pay that knowledge forward." Volunteers act as moderators and open up the chat feature two or three times a day to take questions from the adoring fans of the eagle family.

When I first started watching the SWFEC, I avoided following along with the chat feature. It seemed like a lot of one-timers, asking the same questions over and over again. *When will the eggs hatch? Is that Harriet or M15 on the nest? How big is the nest? Are those bugs in the nest?! When will the eggs hatch? Do the eagles sleep at night? Do eagles have noses? What kind of fish is Harriet eating? When will the eggs hatch!* But eventually, I started to recognize the names of some of the moderators who were patiently and repeatedly answering viewers' questions. I began to appreciate the friendly tone used by the mods, often punctuated with smiley face emojis. It seemed like they'd developed a protocol for handling questions as a team, and two to three moderators were always present on the chat to handle the sheer volume of questions asked. I started to feel like an insider when I could anticipate their responses. The mods made it a point to use the chatters' usernames in their responses. Samour17 answered: "Hi Julie. The eggs of a bald eagle typically begin to hatch 35 days after they are laid. Of course, this is an average and these eggs could hatch sooner or later than 35 days. ☺"

I was also able to send questions to a few volunteers via email through Ginnie. MsSmith57, a volunteer since the first live streaming season (in 2012), was a watcher and a chatter on other bald eagle websites further north before joining the team at SWFEC. "I am originally from Florida and thought how wonderful to watch a southern Bald Eagle nest! One where they're not buried in snow, to observe the difference. Took that look and I was hooked!" she explained. MsSmith57 and the other volunteers are all incredibly knowledgeable about bald eagles, and I have never seen a chatter ask a question they couldn't answer. "We have a great team of moderators that all have a huge thirst for knowledge. Over the years many have studied them by cams and joined in discussions, attended seminars and reading as much as possible" wrote MsSmith57. "Answering a question and [having] someone say 'Oh I had no idea!' or just knowing you helped someone learn something new that day" is MsSmith57's favorite part about volunteering with SWFEC.

Every one of the volunteers contributes to the experience of the viewer in some way, whether it's answering questions in the chat sessions, providing hourly Nest Activity notes in the forum, writing a weekly blog post (called "Nest Notes"), playing the role of "Zoomie," or by physically visiting the nest site daily to take photographs and video footage.

One volunteer who visits the eagle family almost every day is Wskrsnwings. Part of my experience watching Harriet and M15 roosting their eggs every day also involves waiting for Wskrsnwings to upload her morning video footage to YouTube and watching it to see if I've missed anything exciting throughout the day. Almost all of her videos are recorded in the mornings and start with her voice announcing the day and date.

Harriet is known for her "morning vocals" where she screeches from the nest tree, letting everyone know she is awake.[3] Wskrsnwings often talks to the eagles and encourages them, never censoring her emotions or reactions as things happen on and around the nest. Many viewers, including myself, feel as though we are living vicariously through her experiences at the nest. One viewer who goes by the screen name lplzydeco wrote this about Wskrsnwings on the public forum: "I look forward to every one of the videos by Wskrsnwings with her gentle voice and beautiful narratives. She has a way of saying aloud just what I am thinking moment by moment during the watching. She is a treasure!"

Like MsSmith57, Wskrsnwings started getting involved with SWFEC in 2012. She started chatting with the other viewers and offered to take on the role of volunteer. "I love eagles, all birds, and wildlife. As a child, I never saw an eagle due to the effect that DDT had on their population. When I first visited the nest the last week of October 2012 and saw Harriet standing in the nest, I wanted to tell the world about her. I decided to do videos so I could tell viewers what I was seeing, so we could all learn about eagles together," wrote Wskrsnwings. The drive to provide educational experiences for fledgling eagle lovers and love for the eagles are what keep her going back to the nest each season, as much as possible, sometimes twice a day for several hours at a time.

On December 31, 2016, E9[4] the baby eaglet hatched at 7:33 a.m. E9 hatched from the second egg that Harriet laid. Unfortunately, the first egg never hatched and was eventually buried in the nest. The eaglets are not given names ("E" stands for eaglet and 9 means this is the ninth eaglet at this nest since the nest has been monitored) because the Pritchetts want viewers to remember that these are wild creatures, not pets.

I have tuned in every day since December 27 to check in on the eagles. Some days, I might quickly pull up the live stream on

3. wskrsnwings, *SWFL Eagles_A Foggy Start Means More Time With Beautiful Harriet 12-22-16*, 2016, https://www.youtube.com/watch?v=mq6mYQpZsvA.

4. The sex of E9 is unknown but many volunteers and viewers speculate that he is male because of his smaller size. I've developed the habit of referring to him as male, too.

my phone between classes, just to see if there's any cause for concern or new milestones reached by E9. Most days, I have the live feed up on my second monitor in my office at home and even if I'm not focused on it, I turn my volume up so I can listen for Harriet's screeches or E9's squeaks. My desk faces a window and gives me a view of an empty field where I watch a flock of little egrets that are often around, looking for food. The nest tree is near a road, so the traffic sounds mingle with the traffic sounds from nearby Johnston Street and the songs from the little birds who perch in the nest tree get picked up by the camera.

I've watched E9 grow from a little gray fluff-ball into an awkward, downy-headed tween that poops on his mom, to a sleek black fledgling that bravely sleeps away from the nest but always returns for dinner. Most of the time, tuning in to check on the eagles and watching them go about their eagle business is a source of comfort for me. I can tune out all the other noise in the world, and focus on these amazing creatures that are doing what they do. Ginnie mentioned in her email that she talks about the experience of watching the eagles a lot with the other volunteers. "Not only is it a good distraction from life's every day monotony, it also shows life from a new perspective, maybe giving people hope, new feelings for love, and shows perseverance."

As a full-time student and teacher, it is difficult for me to find time to get outside. I've lived in cities of various sizes for most of my life since 2001 and despite a brief spell of thinking I could be a city dweller, I've wanted to live in or near the woods again ever since I moved out of my parents' house. My urge to explore the woods hasn't dwindled since childhood. I used to ride the bus home from school when I was an elementary student and stare out the window for the entire hour ride. Every time we passed a wooded area, I'd picture myself walking through it over tree roots and dirt, touching each tree trunk and listening for nearby woodland creatures. I still do this on car rides (when not driving). Tuning in to see the eagles is a strange, 21st century version of walking in the woods for me. It's meditative but also thoughtful. I think differently when watching the eagles. I think about how feathers work, what nutrients a fish has, the engineering involved in building a nest from sticks and grasses, the way a tree is the perfect home for a bird in a way that blows my mind if I think about it too hard. I think about how miraculous it is that an eagle pair would know exactly what to do when raising their young, happily sacrificing their own comfort in a rain storm to cover their baby who is really too big to fit under them anymore, but tries his best.

After about 13 weeks of watching this eagle family daily, I've begun to get to know them. Harriet is the boss and the oldest, at approximately 20 years of age. She has raised many eaglets in her time, and she knows how to get it done. As MsSmith57 wrote about Harriet, "She's got it all under control." She's tough, and while she made meal times as easy as possible on baby E9, she started making tween-age E9 work for his food by not offering it to him, forcing him to steal bites from her. This has trained E9 to steal the entire fish when it arrives to the nest and mantle it (use his body to cover the fish), nipping at Mom or Dad's toes until they leave the nest. This is an important skill to learn because once E9 leaves the nest, he will depend on carrion or stealing other eagle's food to survive until he masters hunting for himself. When E9 was younger, Harriet would often steal fish from M15 as soon as he brought them to the nest to feed her baby.

M15 is a relatively young eagle of 7 years who has only been Harriet's mate for the past two seasons, including the current season. Described by Wskrsnwings as "ambitious, determined and loving" M15 is an excellent hunter, often bringing fish, squirrel, rabbits, small birds, and opossums to the nest multiple times a day for Harriet and E9. He is patient with E9, taking his nips and impatient squees over food with no complaints. Both adults took turns incubating the eggs and M15 often brought Harriet a fish meal while she was taking her turn on the nest. The two adult eagles are devoted to each other, sleeping side by side perched in the nest tree at night. When E9 was still little, Harriet would sleep in the nest with him and M15 would perch just above them on a tree branch, keeping watch. Even though bald eagles only lay eggs once a year, they continue to "bond" with each other. Harriet has

Nature's *Healing Spirit*

been seen delivering a little kick to M15's side when she wants to bond with him, and he rarely ignores her advances.

Wskrsnwings described E9 as "such a cutie, curious, eager." E9 is certainly curious, brave, smart, and demanding. He watches his parents' every move and learns quickly. When he reaches a new milestone like walking upright on his legs in the nest (eaglets walk on their hocks until their legs gain strength), "wingercizing" for longer periods of time (flapping his wings to strengthen them), learning to grab sticks in the nest with his beak and claws, branching, and finally fledging, the viewers of the SWFEC (including myself) express pride and excitement but also a little sadness. Once E9 leaves the nest area for good to find his own territory, it is likely he will never return. If he does return, he may be treated as an intruder by his parents.

The moderators sympathize with first-time viewers like me who suffer a lot of anxiety over that day when we tune in to find no sign of E9. The nest has seen a relatively successful season this year despite the fact that the first egg did not hatch. In the past, eaglets have died due to unknown causes. E8 and E7 were knocked off a branch they were perched on by an owl one night, resulting in a broken leg for E8. When something like this happens to one of the eagles, the Pritchett family contacts CROW (Clinic for the Rehabilitation of Wildlife) to help. Between CROW and the Florida Fish and Wildlife Conservation Commission, a decision is made concerning whether or not human intervention would benefit the eagles. E8 was found on the ground after falling and taken in for rehabilitation because he was otherwise perfectly healthy and would be able to contribute to the bald eagle population after his leg healed. CROW also stepped in when Ozzie, Harriet's first mate was injured by another bald eagle (believed to be M15!). Unfortunately, they were not able to save Ozzie[5] and he passed away. Though I never knew Ozzie, he was incredibly popular with viewers and moderators.

---

5. Here's a hilarious video of Ozzie on the nest with Harriet and eaglets. Harriet feeds the eaglets while Ozzie catches his reflection in the camera. https://www.youtube.com/watch?v=aijJsYBVpXM

"I was crushed when Ozzie died," wrote Wskrsnwings. "But I thought about how much he taught me about the day-to-day life of eagles. And I watched Harriet in her resilience go on and fulfill what she and Ozzie and all other eagles' one goal in life is—procreation of their species."

There is a video on YouTube of Ozzie removing the body of one of his deceased eaglets from the nest. It's awful to watch, but I made myself do it in an attempt to remind myself that these creatures are not my pets.

MsSmith57 also grieved the loss of Ozzie and the eaglets that didn't make it. "It's hard, very hard. Being a moderator during the loss of an eagle or eaglet is like losing a family member, but you try to keep the tears in check to read the comments and answer questions and try to still make sense! Over and over seemingly unending sadness. It takes a toll for sure. But it's what we do. You have to take a break often when those things happen. The viewers feel it just as much and you kind of relive it with each one. Losing a couple eaglets here was so difficult but Ozzie was a real heartbreaker. I adored him as did so many. He was special. And actually no more special than most male eagles at every nest, they're all special to someone. Harriet would give him what for and he still went about his duties as he is programmed by nature to do. To this day I cannot watch a video or see a picture of Oz without tearing up. Knowing how hard and harsh their life can be you try to not get emotional, that's almost impossible to accomplish! They steal your heart. Watching the good stuff though makes up for the losses in a way, it's pure joy."

The Pritchett family has been pressured in the past to turn the cams off, especially when the young eaglet died of natural causes and was decomposing in the nest. "In my opinion, it goes against what we stand for, which is education and learning. In the end we crafted a statement to help with this issue and it has gotten us through some tough times and emotional viewers," Ginnie wrote. The statement, located on the live feed webpage, states, "Eagles are wild birds and anything can happen in the wild. The Southwest Florida Eagle Camera (SWFEC) does not interfere or intervene and allows nature to take its course. You will see life and you might see death, but this is nature at her finest."

So, on January 30th when M15 was gone from the nest almost the entire day, viewers (including myself) were full of worry. It was the first time he'd been absent this long all season. Moderators attempted to calm our fears by putting out messages in chat and the forum saying that sometimes eagles have difficult hunting days and not to worry. Of course, viewers were making all kinds of speculations in the chat, and I couldn't stop myself from reading them. Maybe M15 got in a fight with another eagle and was injured somewhere. Maybe he'd been hit by a car (there is a busy road near the nest). M15 is the main provider of food for both Harriet and E9. While Harriet is certainly capable of hunting, her main role is to protect E9 while M15 is out hunting.

More worries surfaced as the day wore on. *What if M15 is injured or worse and Harriet has to go hunting, leaving E9 vulnerable?* As the hours passed and E9 went longer and longer without food, I became more and more frantic. I logged on to chat in the afternoon, hoping to hear some good news or see that the banner at the top of the website had been updated with a feeding. But no, no fish for E9 since 8:30 that morning and no sign of M15. The moderators continued to try and calm everyone, assuring us that E9 still had food in his crop (a pouch in the esophagus that stores food when the stomach is full[6]) from the morning fish meal. I had to shut my computer off. I was terrified. What was I thinking, getting so attached to these birds? How had this happened?

Finally, later that evening, M15 did return to the nest (I know because I couldn't help but check back in). Although he didn't have a fish for E9, he looked unharmed so that was a relief. He brought five fish to the nest throughout the next day, so he certainly made up for his bad hunting luck. E9 was in no danger of starving and Harriet would have provided for him. This was the first time I heard the saying "Trust the Eagles" from the mods. It has become a sort of mantra for new viewers and myself who are now

---

6. "Bald Eagle's Diet and Feeding Habits - American Bald Eagle Information," accessed March 24, 2017, http://www.baldeagleinfo.com/eagle/eagle3.html.

experiencing a fledgling E9.

On March 14th, at approximately 7:22 a.m., he fell from a branch he was perched on. In the week prior to his "fledging incident," E9 had been eagerly learning to branch, which is when the eaglet leaves the nest and perches on a nearby branch in the nest tree. He was only branching on nearby limbs, so he wasn't officially flying yet. I was ridiculously proud of him. He would hop from one branch, back to the nest, to another branch with such confidence. Until he slipped.

I didn't actually see the fall, but saw video footage taken by Wskrsnwings[7] later. In the video, E9 hops and just misses the edge of the nest. He ends up hanging upside down underneath it, claws clinging to the branches sticking out of the nest. There's a moment in the video when it looks like he decides to just let go, because he knows he can't recover from that position. As he falls, E9 bumps along the tree trunk and then seems to remember he has wings. It looks like he starts to fly a little. Harriet swoops down, too, but the camera loses focus. Wskrsnwings zooms in on an eagle in a nearby tree, but it turns out to be Harriet. Her voice is full of panic when she realizes she's lost sight of E9. A white truck goes by on the farm's access road, right in front of the nest tree where E9 was last sighted and Wskrsnwings can be heard saying "Please stop!" as she is certain the truck will hit E9. Thankfully, she catches him again in the lens of her camera and he seems unhurt, standing in the grass near the nest tree.

About a half an hour after the fall happened, I tuned in from my phone while I was still lying in bed, trying to wake up, with no sense of what I was about to see. The video footage showed an empty nest. I switched to Cam 2, thinking he was just on a branch in the nest tree, and that's when I saw him. He was perched on a nearby fence. Imagine the shock of seeing this baby so far from where you last saw him when you checked in on him before falling asleep the night before.

---

7. A video taken and narrated by Wskrsnwings the moment E9 accidentally fledged. Skip to 3:22 for the fall: wskrsnwings, *SWFL Eagles_Accidental Fledge For 73 Day Old E9~7:22AM~03-14-17*, 2017, https://www.youtube.com/watch?v=JFpU9KPRn3I.

I hurried to my computer to get on the forum. People were reporting that E9 didn't seem to be injured in the fall. He was now exploring on the ground near the fence. I could see a crowd of people from Cam 1, with cameras at the ready. I had to shower and head to campus, so I tore myself away from the computer. Later, when I was able to check in, E9 was no longer within range of any of the cameras. There was nothing to be done except repeatedly refresh the forum and watch the chat to see if someone had any news to report. I kept telling myself to trust the eagles, but it seemed so impossible for a creature that was a fuzzy, wobbly little baby fresh from the egg only 73 days ago to survive by itself. Eaglets typically fledge between 9 and 10 weeks of age[8], and E9 was 10 weeks old, but I wasn't ready to see him so far away from the nest. I was supposed to be reading for a class, but I was glued to that website. I read on the forum that Harriet and M15 brought E9 a fish on the ground earlier. It was reassuring to know that the parents knew where E9 was.

Throughout that day and the day following, viewers and moderators reported sightings of E9 who seemed to be having a great time exploring and taking little flights all over the property. Even though his wings weren't that strong yet, he managed to make it up to a tree branch near the nest tree. I was watching the cams the evening of March 15 and witnessed his triumphant return flight to the nest, where a fish was waiting for him. It was beautiful. I may have cried a little. I definitely clapped. The next day, Wskrsnwings posted the video she'd taken when E9 fell from the nest and I watched it for the first time, feeling panic and worry all over again.

Since then, E9 has been boldly flying from tree to tree all over the Pritchett property, venturing down to the pond, checking out the ducks and horses. He continues to return to the nest tree each night and throughout the day for a fish meal from Dad. Eventually, he will go with his parents on hunting trips to learn those skills and practice stealing. Then, like all the other eaglets from this nest, he

---

8. "Slide 1 - Eaglefacts.pdf," accessed March 14, 2017, https://www.fws.gov/uploadedfiles/region_5/nwrs/central_zone/montezuma/eaglefacts.pdf.

will leave for good one day. I can't say how I'll handle that when it happens, but right now I am thankful that he still likes to plop down in the nest and screech for food.

PATTI JEANE PANGBORN is a PhD student at the University of Louisiana at Lafayette, studying English with a concentration in Creative Writing. She holds an MFA in poetry from Columbia College Chicago. Her poems have appeared in *Columbia Poetry Review* issue 27 and *Shadowgraph Quarterly*. She is originally from Michigan.

The Worst Thing That Happened

by Lee del Rosso

I stepped off of the wooden walkway, my feet hitting chilly sand. Just ahead, the vast indigo ocean beckoned. Intoxicated by its beauty, I breathed in deeply and then exhaled. I could smell, could taste the fall coming, and it felt exhilarating. A few hours ago, the Long Island sun had been overpowering, and the crowds of people had impeded any walking I wanted to do. It seemed millions of rambunctious children were everywhere, watched over by cranky adults, disgruntled by too much sun, sea, and Labor Day beer. Now, the beach was all but deserted, save for what looked like a father and his three young daughters at the shoreline, still aching for a swim, their towels and things in a pile behind them.

This was the time I liked the beach best, just after dusk, with a fiery sinking sun to the west, and the leaching of all color, leaving only the palest shade of gray in the east. There is comfort for me in this particular kind of isolation, and I have never felt afraid on a deserted beach. I don't swim in the Long Beach waters at night, though, because the darker it gets, the more the waves resemble long, black, white-tipped fingers, eager to pull me down with their undertow.

We had arrived at the cabanas later than planned, which turned out to be a good thing. At a particular point in the late afternoon, suddenly everyone departed, off to other parties or barbecues. No more baseball games broadcast from radios. No more crying children. I could hear the gulls again.

Sitting across from me at one of the sun-bleached picnic tables, Miguel, my brother-in-law and a school psychologist, asked what I would be teaching my writing students at Berkeley business college for the last two weeks of the quarter now that I was decamping for NYU (New York University). I told him about the class's last topic, which was to write an essay about something that had changed them.

There was one student, a Dominican woman named Nina, who had joined the class quite late: a month into the quarter. Nina was a heavy woman, not very tall, and about twenty-five years old. She was a single mother with a two-year-old daughter. Her essay described being sexually abused by her father from the age of two, which robbed her of the ability to speak, just like the author Maya Angelou.

Months passed before her mother took Nina to a doctor, who discovered sores on her mouth and vagina. When he told Nina's mother he suspected abuse, she responded by saying that could not possibly happen in her house. The abuse continued until Nina was three-and-a-half.

At that time, the family moved to the United States, living in an apartment so small that everyone slept in the same bed: her mother, father, Nina and her younger brother. Still Nina did not speak. Her father had been selling drugs to support the family, and Nina still does not know exactly what happened, but one night her father was doing something behind the house, and when he came in, her mother screamed at him, slapped him in the face and threw him out.

After many months passed, and Nina was sure he was not coming back, she began speaking, both in Spanish and English.

She ended her essay with something like, "I can finally talk about it; I can finally speak."

Miguel cleared his throat. He had his arms folded and a pained look on his face.

I said, "I don't know, Miguel, but when I finished that essay, I wished I had a degree in another subject that would have been more helpful, or..." I paused, studying my hands for a moment before meeting his gaze again. "Or I wished that I was you."

He laughed, asking then, "How did you respond to her?"

I explained that Nina had passed in her essay late, after the term had ended, so I critiqued her over the phone. It was extremely well-written. Then, because I had to say something about what had happened to her, and I guessed the answer was no, I asked if she had sought counseling. She said her friends had suggested it, and she knew the weight correlated to the abuse, *Blah, blah, blah*, she said, but no. No counseling.

I strongly suggested it as well, and from a specialist in sexual abuse and incest. I told her that whatever happened to keep writing, not as therapy but to make sense of what happened to her. She said she had been through a lot in her life, and I said it seemed so. It was her ambition to write a book before her life was over, and I told her she definitely had one in her, and that she's a wonderful writer.

I related to Miguel, "In a split second, two things occurred to me. That this was the first time in ten weeks Nina sounded confident, like she was on a path and knew where she wanted to go. But it was odd for her, at twenty-five, to use the words, *before my life is over*. Then she said to me, '*I tested positive*.' I asked her, 'Positive for what?' And she told me HIV. She found out when she was pregnant."

Reliving the moment, I looked out to the sea, hearing the waves breathing in the distance.

I told Miguel that I could not bring myself to ask whether her daughter was positive or not. "Instead, I said something like..."

"Oh!" Miguel said.

I shrugged. "That's right. 'Oh!' is exactly what I said. I got off the phone with her, and I just wanted... I wanted..." I shook my head. What I had done for Nina was nothing.

"Well," Miguel said, "You encouraged her to keep writing, and to get counseling. You gave her permission to write about it, a safe place where she can go to, yes, to make sense of what happened to her. Or, to just get it out so she doesn't have to hold onto it."

I was silent. To me, it sounded puny.

Clearly reading my thoughts, Miguel continued, "Believe me, in my job, I wish I had the power to do more than I can do. You know?"

It was then I went for a walk.

Standing on the shore, I tiptoed to the water, then raced back to the sand as the incoming tide chased me, a game I used to play as a child that made me breathless with laughter. It was coming in fast.

A few feet away from me, the three girls, in the water now, jumped up and down, splashing each other, shrieking. They climbed all over their father, intent on mock-drowning the poor man. Despite being outnumbered, he was laughing.

Suddenly, I saw the pile of towels and clothes that the family had left once-safely on shore slide by me, lifted by water. One more wave, and their belongings would be gone. I raced in to save them, and in the process, lost the game. The tide had won. But the girls ran toward me, squealing. "Thank you! Thank you so much!"

"Thank you," their father said, sounding relieved.

"No problem," I replied.

As I turned to walk further on down the shore, I heard one of the young girls say to the other, "Wow, that would have been the worst thing ever, right? If we had lost our stuff?"

"Yeah," the other girl said, "I don't care about the towel but my favorite tee shirt I just got and the other stuff—that would have been the worst."

I continued walking, my soaked shorts clammy against my skin. I thought about what the girls had said. I thought about Nina.

I thought about fathers and daughters.

The chill in the air had gotten sharper and there was a wind that no longer belonged to summer. I looked up. The stars were appearing, nudging out the red, bloody sky.

LEE DEL ROSSO originally trained as a classical singer and completed a post-graduate program at LAMDA (London Academy of Music and Dramatic Art), living and performing in London before moving to New York City. Her plays "Clare's Room," and "Samaritan," have been performed off-Broadway and had public readings, while "St. John," her third play, was a semi-finalist for the 2011 Eugene O'Neill National Playwrights Conference. Her writing has appeared in *The New York Times, Barking Sycamores Neurodivergent Literature, Razor's Edge Literary Magazine, The Literary Traveler, Serving House Journal, VietnamWarPoetry, Young Minds Magazine* (London/UK), *Time Out New York, The Huffington Post, The Neue Rundschau* (Germany), *Jetlag Café* (Germany), and *One Magazine* (London/UK), for whom she writes theater reviews. She teaches writing at New York University.

March Bird Song

by Sharon Mack

My granddaughter of seven years and eleven months stands next to me by the open screen door, hugging herself as the March chill rolls by. She's whistling at a blue jay who is sitting high in the birch tree calling for a mate. She whistles twice, and the blue jay almost seems to answer her. She whistles again and this time she is certain he answers her. She slowly smiles, her eyes widening in surprise. "Can't we record this?" she says. "These sounds would be so nice to fall asleep to."

On our little hill in Maine, in our wide backyard by the edge of the woods across from the river, the birds returned from their winter vacation earlier this week. It was instantaneous. Sudden. Like that moment when the Jack-In-The-Box explodes; quiet—flip a switch—raucous. All winter, the silence rolled in with the morning fog or flew in on the snow and sleet. It held on tightly one crisp frozen day after another, and thudded down at night. But on this day, the air is suddenly alive, filled with cheeps and beautiful songs and desperate calls for partners. It is as if a new family with endless children moved into the neighborhood in the night, bringing life back to the tired houses and empty trees. Or as if the school playground that stood so forlorn and quiet has burst open at the sound of the bell.

The blue jays are calling back and forth across the yard. "I'm available," they screech, while the fat bellied juncos and the flitting chickadees and the small sparrows and pudgy wrens bombard the bird feeders and dance on the soft ground where the seed has fallen. The robins strut about on patches of barren ground where the snow has melted, hustling for a few steps, stopping to listen for tricky little worms, and then hustling forward again. The gang of widowed mourning doves has returned too, like a row of gossiping old ladies sitting on the wire that feeds the cable to my house. Shoulder to shoulder, they softly carry stories. I wonder if it is the aerial version of the game, Mouse, and if the story told by the first dove is vastly different than the one heard by the last.

In their frenzy at the feeders, three yellow finches hit the living room window within an hour. The action outside reminded me of old black and white newsreels of World War I bombing raids, the feathered bodies buzzing the sky in dogfights—all movement and finesse, feet tucked up, wings extended, heads pushed forward. The underside of their wings is so extraordinarily beautiful in flight, as they whirl and bank, a dance choreographed by instinct. A ballet. Except when the reflection of sun and sky off the window appears as a mirage, tricking their sense of flight. Little crash landings are happening. No broken wings or necks. Yet.

My granddaughter reports that the noisy blue jay in the birch tree is now joined by another that flew across the yard from an exceptionally tall pine, answering his call for a wife. "They will pick out their nest now," she says. She stands quietly in the chilly doorway, watching, listening as the newly paired-up jays fly off together.

"When they find each other, are they happy?" she asks.

"Of course," I say. "Now they are a family."

"But why do they stop singing then?" she asks. And I say I don't know, but that it could be that sometimes, even when you have the very thing you work so hard to get, you forget to sing its praises.

You forget to be grateful and you forget to tell each other how happy you make each other and how magical it was when you found each other and how important you are in each other's lives. She hugs herself a bit tighter and thinks about this.

"You make me happy," she says quietly, looking up at me with eyes that mirror mine.

And a little song begins its tune in my heart. My own spring bird song—swirling flutes and violins around me. Cellos and timpani under my feet, oboes in my hair. If I open my mouth, cartoon-sized musical notes will fly out and encompass this child and me as my heart song fills my house, my yard, the woods and then continues floating down the river, rolling to the sea, where it is carried endlessly by the wind.

SHARON MACK is a retired journalist living on the bold coast of Downeast Maine. After 35 years of telling other people's stories, she is now telling her own. She has been previously published in *Left Hook, The Feminine Collective, 3 Nation Anthology, Working Waterfront* and *The Bangor Daily News*. She won the 2017 Prize in Prose Award from the *Five80Split* Literary and Arts Journal.

Moonwoman

by Marilyn Sequoia

Have you seen
The woman in the moon,
When she lights
The whole night sky?

Have you seen
The gleaming white
Plate of her face,
The mounds above her eyes?

No mascara dark lids,
Or cherry-ripe cheeks.
No grinning pink lips,
No ringlets, no wisps.

She wears instead
Her wig of clouds
On a proudly
Balded head.

Her sisters below
Find solace there
For the loss of their own
Breasts and hair.

Her mouth forms an oh!
In caressing compassion:
These women she heals,
With her tears to the sea

This madame
This mentor
This woman
This moon.

MARILYN SEQUOIA is a poet living in Riverside, CA. In addition to her own chapbook *New Wilderness*, Marilyn Sequoia's poems may be found in Habitat for Humanity's *Raising the Roof*, in C.G. Jung Club's "The Orange Circle," in UC Riverside's Literary Journal *Mosaic*, in the anthology *Discovering the Spirit of Place*, and in Katya Williamson's book: *Bringing the Soul Back Home* (Compass Books, 2009). Over the years, nature and music have been Ms. Sequoia's primary sources of joy and hope.

The Bottom of the Barrel

by Larissa Hikel

When it was over, I would lull myself to sleep thinking about revenge. More correctly, I thought of vivid revenges and then rejected them. Almost every idea was quickly followed by a reason not to, and in this way, I fell asleep many times without resolving anything.

I don't know when the crow discovered the rain barrel; last year it used the bird bath. The bird's habits were a surprise, I hadn't known.

Peanut shells were ever-present. A few times the year before, I was surprised by a bright blue robin's egg, and on one notable occasion, a dead rodent lying face down in the water. I'm not sure what kind.

Those items I removed to the garbage can, with a hand encased in a plastic bag from Shopper's Drug Mart, before rinsing and re-filling the bird bath. I did not want to be left alone, or deprived of the crow's beauty.

Trying to fall asleep again, I did a few revision exercises.

Fire was too dangerous, as was tampering with his vehicle.... I hoped he'd die, but what if he had a passenger or hit someone?

What if he ran over his neighbor's cat or children? I couldn't risk it. A few times I cried. I imagined his lawn, his mailbox, his doorstep. Flaming bag of shit?

Too obvious.

Though it is suddenly and clearly also too obvious, what a bag of shit he is, if not literally.

In the morning, I notice the water in the rain barrel is brightly colored. There is a red ring around it on the inside, just above the water level.

That first winter, when it was colder than Mars, I would leave my cozy apartment deep in the frigid night to meet him and his dog on the frozen river.

Sometimes, I would later receive a Haiku:

Magical mermaid,
swimming in a turbulent sea,
spies lone Unicorn.

I received good night messages complete with Xs and Os, and once a pink t-shirt printed with morning glories and yes, a unicorn, that I wore to sleep.

The area surrounding the rain barrel is littered suddenly one afternoon with what looks like spit-out clumps of down and small multicolored feathers.

That summer, I rode my bike over under the moonlight.

He played Turkish pop music on his little boom box. I'm not sure, but the music may have been on a cassette tape. There was a patterned scarf like a kaleidoscope covering his bedroom window, and one wall of the room was painted an ugly brown.

When I asked if he was going to finish painting the room, he looked at me in disdain and let me know, "It's an accent wall."

His dog slept on top of my discarded clothing.

One morning his phone made a noise; he picked it up off the bedside table and looked at it, then typed a response. His shoulder was touching mine. He said, "Are you reading over my shoulder?" I could not reply. My mouth was filled with beaks and talons.

Silently I stared at the accent wall while he got out of bed. He went down the stairs to the floor below where the bathroom was, to take a shower.

I looked at his phone; I read the message, and the messages before it.

Unlocking my bike, my hands shook, and I could feel my teeth vibrating the whole way home.

He sent me a text message: *Did I offend you somehow, or did you have things to do?*

My reply: *Stay on your side of the river*

A moment passed, then a response: *Wow*

Wow is right, I typed.

I stayed in bed the rest of the day.

The crow sits on the edge of the barrel when it looks down. I too gaze deeply into the still surface of the dark red water.

A floating eyeball.

Via text message: *A picture of a carved wooden mermaid, a statue. Her wavy hair disappearing into the grain of the wood. She looks like you.*

I returned to the room with the accent wall.

In the morning I saw that a black polyester satin robe with a floral pattern hung over the closet door.

He was still asleep. I stretched my legs, turned onto my side and touched his ankle with my foot.

His voice: "Don't!"
The sound startled me.
"You're a pest," he said.

The crow has left a corpse dissected on the top of the pipe that drains water from the roof into the rain barrel. It is baking in the heat. I hope the rain eventually washes it off or at least softens it.

I thought about the phone, the cheap fabric of the floral robe, the accent wall.

I'm a pest.

The corpse sat on the drain pipe all afternoon, drying in the sun. Some of the parts that had once been inside were missing. The crow has taken the heart. I wonder if it is a gift for someone, or has simply been eaten.

Still and silent, the water is holding many secrets only the crow knows.

This cannot continue.

There is no other way. I tip the barrel over and watch the water begin to gush out onto the grass.

By the half empty point, the pouring water begins to fill with small objects, bits of sodden fur and feathers, tiny bones and feet, and finally, the eye ball.

The smell is overpowering. For a moment I think I will vomit onto the lawn, but I back up a few paces to breathe in some fresher air and manage to finish the job.

I think about phrases I have heard, such as 'pay with your life.'

I wish I could make someone pay with his life. I wish I could cut his throat and wipe the blood off my blade using his hair.

I picture putting the feet into a little envelope. I imagine placing the envelope gently under his pillow. I imagine sealing it with a kiss.

By now everyone has heard the story of the girl who fed the crows, and was given gifts by them, glittering trinkets for thank you.

Well, I gave the crow water in a barrel, and received a much different gift.

The crow eats many things, picking them apart and washing the individual fragments.

I'd given him a jigsaw puzzle from my childhood that depicts a river running through a park, all the animals of the ark and some magical creatures, including both a Mermaid and a Unicorn, flying a kite.

I am a pest.

What if I made a casserole or baked a cake? I picture him vomiting up the little bones and the surprise on his face.

I imagine carefully setting the bits of fur, guts and bones into a little pile and setting it on fire.

Placing the eyeball on top of the pyre, and when everything has been reduced to dust, putting that dust in a jar, putting the jar in my backpack, biking across the bridge to his house, and blowing that dust across his lawn to his doorstep, into his windows.

Stringing the eyeball onto a piece of thread, and tying it to his door knob.

I'm watching you. Well I'm not watching you, I've seen you.

All the way down to the bottom.

LARISSA HIKEL is a freelance writer from Winnipeg, MB. She brings a native instinct to her writing, photography and acting. She explores the world from a personally complex place. High school drop-out, drifter, used to being a chameleon, able to shift between identities as they serve her, she has the power to observe life from a wide range of vantage points which she brings to her art.

The Queensland Vine

by Blaise Allen

Two years of faith.
Daily watering and feeding
of bare sticks, our Florida
Wisteria finally took root.

From climbing wooden vines,
bright lavender-blue stars cascade
around the roof. An entire cosmos
of five-pointed flowers orbit the house.

This spring blooms new
galaxies in the dark corner
by the kitchen window. Purple
meteors. Violet, ultraviolet corona.

After a week, the flowers fade
jade green, then become white
Dwarf stars.
Shooting stars.
Falling Stars.
Constellations, guide us home.

BLAISE ALLEN, Ph.D., is a Licensed Clinical Social Worker, and Director of Community Outreach for the Palm Beach Poetry Festival. Her poems have been widely published in literary anthologies and journals. Blaise bridges her passion of social welfare and the arts through community engagement and project management.

River Magic

by Diane Byington

We put in near Blue Spring State Park, which is a manatee refuge on the St. John's River in Central Florida. I settle onto my Wilderness ten-foot-long kayak that fits me like an extension of my own body. My husband climbs into his considerably larger Hobie, which allows him to pedal as well as paddle. He's planning on fishing while I observe nature and hope to see a manatee.

But it's late March, one of the first hot, muggy days of the season. The thousand-pound manatees that spend the winters gliding just under the river's surface have probably already made their way out to the colder waters of the ocean. I wouldn't blame them. But this is the first afternoon I've been able to take away from work in months, so I am hopeful but not optimistic.

It's the way I feel about my marriage.

Every year, my husband and I run away from our problems and spend the winter in our retirement haven, a double-wide trailer perched beside a beautiful lake in Central Florida. We've always had our best times on vacation, and this feels like a four-months-long vacation. That is, until we begin to think about going back to our real lives. And then the weight of our upcoming return to reality makes us both cranky.

We are hoping for a good day, a reminder of why we are together. So we paddle upstream first, planning to drift back downstream when we are tired. A short way upstream is the run to Blue Spring. The water's year-round 73 degrees lures manatees in the colder months, and tubers and swimmers the rest of the year. We slide over a rope stretched across the entrance and glance at a sign that warns away fishermen and motorboats. My husband pulls in his fishing line and we paddle in to explore.

On the way to the spring, the water is deep and clear, like a natural aquarium. Some of the fish swimming beneath our kayaks are five feet long or more, with pointed noses. Gar, I think they're called. Others look more like regular fish, with rounded noses. These might be mullet. But I see no manatees, and neither have any of the tourists strolling along the boardwalk beside the stream. The day isn't over though.

We return to the river and my husband lets out his fishing line again. The current is just strong enough to require us to paddle every few seconds if we want to get anywhere. But there's no place to go, really. The banks as far as we can see are covered with trees and brush in myriad shades of green. I recognize palm trees, of course, and cypress and oaks, but nothing else. I paddle haphazardly and try to stay out of the way of the rental boats and tandem kayaks that race by me. Signs posted on tree trunks warn boaters to make no wake, because this is a manatee zone. Except that it isn't, at least not on this day. Maybe the boat drivers don't notice the signs.

We turn off onto a branch, a loop that my husband has seen on his phone's GPS. The other kayaks and motorboats don't bother, so we have the place to ourselves. He wants to stop and fish, so I rest my paddle across my legs. I spend the next half hour trying to describe the color of the new leaves on the cypress trees. I don't come up with much. Spring green. Shamrock green. The green of a shiny new traffic light. None of these pitiful attempts comes close to describing the vibrant color, but it does describe my thinking: slow and relaxed, like the rest of me. I don't particularly care whether I capture the best description for the green. I'm happy just to notice.

Eventually, my husband gives up on fishing and we paddle onward, through a narrowing stream in a forest that could easily harbor Tarzan, or a Bigfoot of the swamp. As a child, one of my favorite television shows was about a ranger who drove an airboat through the Everglades. It could have been filmed here, I think, instead of the real Everglades. I can still hum the theme song. Or is that a different song altogether? I can't remember, and it doesn't matter right now. Unfortunately, Florida has changed since I was a child. The state's natural resources are threatened by pollution, unfettered growth, and global warming. I choose not to worry about those problems today.

Great blue herons stand upright and still as they watch for just the right dinner to swim their way, and then strike in an instant to come up with a wriggling fish. Snake-birds pop their long black necks up from the water and swim for a moment before diving back down. Snowy egrets with question-mark necks fly over. I don't spot any alligators, but I hear their grunts deep in the lily pads. It's mating season, so maybe they are calling for a partner. Or warning me off. My feet are dangling over the edge of the kayak. I make a point to pull them in, safeguard my toes. I've never heard of an alligator bothering a kayaker, but a little caution seems an appropriate response.

On this perfect spring day, a few clouds make for fun watching but don't portend any rain. The wind blows just strongly enough to keep away the mosquitoes. Deep, dark, nearly still water carries me along. There is not a single thing I need to do right now. My bug spray and sunscreen do their work, and my water bottle is within easy reach. I resonate with Huck and Jim, dozing and drifting down the river.

Eventually the loop brings us back to the main river. I'm a bit sorry to return to civilization, or at least to what passes for it on the river. Pre-teen boys pilot their family's rent-a-boats with smug smiles, and drunk men swill beer as they race through the no-wake zones. It is a typical day on the water.

As we drift toward our take-out place, I can't predict how the next months will go, or whether my husband and I will be able to live with our intractable problems, much less overcome them. I can't foresee the future. I just know we both enjoy being on the water, and I'll take this sweet memory back into the real world.

I'm sorry, but not surprised, that I didn't see any manatees on this day. I hope to try again next year, when the cool days and relatively warm spring water invite the giant sea creatures to tarry a while. I'm hopeful, but not optimistic, that my husband and I will make it back here to see them.

DIANE BYINGTON is a social worker and writer who divides her time between Boulder, Colorado and Central Florida. She has published numerous professional articles, half a dozen short stories, and is the author of the novel, *Run Away Home* (Red Adept Publishing, 2018). www.dianebyington.com

Bugs I Have Bashed

by H.L.M. Lee

Years ago, in the era before the internet, one of my high school teachers mentioned the English word "puce" originated from the French word for "flea," and rubbed out an imaginary bug on the blackboard, its blood supposedly that odd grayish-pinkish-purple color. I had always attributed the story to Mrs. Janssen's dry wit and had forgotten about it until I found the same explanation online, reminding me about my fascination with insects.

I grew up in Columbus, Ohio, in a neighborhood of new tract homes that must have been clear cut from the woods that stood only a block away. As a 10-year-old boy I explored them, but never too deeply for fear of becoming lost. One path took me by a pond. The cabin there belonged to a man who, rumor had it, kept his shotgun loaded with rock salt. I never saw him and frequently trespassed, anyway, to catch frogs, turtles and bugs.

At the time I wanted to be an entomologist, a scientist who studies insects, despite being scared out of my wits one day when a cicada (*Magicicada cassini*) landed on my shirt. Looking like a giant fly, it placidly stared at me with ruby eyes, its cellophane-like wings folded over a thick black body only an inch long but seemingly the size of a boxcar. Cicadas spend most of their lives underground as grubs, emerging as adults in vast numbers period-ically every 13 or 17 years, depending on the brood. That summer their constant, ear-splitting whine rose in pitch and volume to a crescendo then diminished only to repeat endlessly during a few humid weeks. The cicada that terrorized me was the first bug I wanted to squash out of malice, but I had enough sense to avoid splattering its considerable guts all over myself, and let it fly away on its own.

During school vacations I often carried a homemade butterfly net, either on my shoulder or raised high like a wind sock. I was never coordinated enough to catch anything on the wing, a tech-nique that required a deft sweep then a flick of the wrist to twist the net closed. Instead, I slapped my net over a resting specimen; though awkward, that move worked well enough.

If I had nothing else to do, I wandered to the pond but could never catch the dragonflies (*Odonata*) hovering there hopelessly out of reach. Fantastically agile flying machines, they zipped back and forth, changing direction and stopping unpredictably in mid-air to feast on midges whirling over the water. The day I found one motionless on a reed, its stiff, intricately veined wings outstretched, I froze and held my breath; any sudden movement would send it darting away. But it was dead, somehow undisturbed and in per-fect condition. With huge eyes faintly stippled, iridescent thorax and long straight abdomen, the dragonfly looked like jewelry. Gin-gerly picking it up, I barely felt the weight of my prize as I carried it home to pin on a board.

Beetles (*Coleoptera*) were much easier to capture than dragon-flies but no less interesting. Glossy with black carapaces, the males sporting mandibles like the antlers of a six-point buck, stag beetles (*Lucanus elephas*) looked threatening but in fact were harmless. Whenever I plucked one off the lawn to show my sisters, they ran screaming inside the house. On summer evenings stolid June bugs (*Pelidnota punctata*), attracted by our lamps, buzzed against the window screens. Like many kids from a certain era, I reserve my fondest memories for fireflies (*Photinus pyralis*), which are beetles despite the name. Reacting luciferin and luciferase, a chemical and an enzyme, in a special abdominal organ, they create their signature bioluminescent glow. I remember muggy nights in July when we drank Coca-Cola floats and chased a dot of yellow light bobbing about the yard. After it disappeared, we veered to pursue other fireflies blinking in response.

Back in those days a certain brand of potato chip came in a large cardboard box, which happened to be a cube a little more than a foot on each side. After cutting panels from it and covering the openings with cellophane wrap, I made a terrarium for keeping live insects. My favorite was the praying mantis (*Mantis religiosa*), found in bushes, camouflaged green and looking like a twig, but a twig with serrated arms that whipped out to grab the insect that would be its next meal. If I placed my hand next to one, I could coax it onto a finger then drop it into a jar. I made the mistake once of putting two in my terrarium at the same time, with sticks and leaf litter covering the floor to resemble a natural environment. The next day only a single mantis remained, somehow looking satiated (if that were even possible), gnawing on a leftover wing.

Of all the insects, butterflies and moths (*Lepidoptera*) seem the most whimsical. Like flowers on the wind, their existence is a gift. Bold, orange monarchs (*Danaus plexippus*), everyone's favorite, gathered around the milkweed down the road. Tiger swallowtails (*Papilio glaucus*) glided into our yard and were buttery yellow with black stripes, not to be confused with the similar zebra swallowtail (*Eurytides marcellus*), which was smaller and white with black stripes. Dusky brown with eye spots, wood nymphs (*Cercyonis pegala*) somehow could fly between the tall, unruly stalks of weeds in those neighborhood woods and were nearly impossible to catch.

One winter, high on a tree branch, I found the cocoon of a cecropia moth (*Hyalophora cecropia*), one of the largest North American moths, nearly the size of a bat. I kept it in my terrarium until spring, when the adult pushed its way out, hung on a branch and unfurled gorgeous chocolate brown wings with prominent red and white markings. I promptly killed it in a jar with gasoline-soaked cotton balls then displayed it in my collection.

That was decades ago. I no longer engage in this kind of extermination, though I admit to swatting mosquitoes (*Anopheles walkeri, Aedes sollicitans* or *Aedes canadenis*) and houseflies (*Musca domestica*). If I could revisit that time, I would only observe, with patience and acuity, the insects I used to collect. Now I catch the errant creepy crawler in a jar to show my daughters before releasing it outside.

Though my town is adjacent to Boston, it has acres of parks and yards full of bushes and trees. I thought diverse insects would fill all that green space—but apparently not. An occasional dragonfly shoots through the neighborhood, perhaps having lost its way from the nearby Muddy River. Ladybugs (*Coccinella novemnotata*) are relatively common and everyone appreciates their charm, but very few large beetles appear. No praying mantises stalk the bushes, and only plain, cabbage white butterflies (*Pieris rapae*) dance by our flowers.

I wonder whether such paucity is true elsewhere. Maybe few suburban areas are near undisturbed woods now. Maybe pesticides have killed off the large, charismatic insects as well as the pests, or global warming has damaged the ecosystem. I don't know, but I am disturbed when reading about honeybee (*Apis mellifera*) dieoffs, which seem to be more evidence of environmental problems.

My wife and I spent our honeymoon in Tuscany fifteen years ago, and I still recall a certain garden where we held hands and time paused. On that warm, sunny day the scent from dense plantings of lavender filled the air, which was thick with bumblebees (*Bombus terricola occidentalis*) bouncing among the flowers. Even now I hear the buzzing and the almost subliminal rhythm as they landed then took flight. When I was standing there with my wife, how different, how silent and vacant would that moment have felt without them?

Every time our family walks through a park, I show my daughters the insects that we encounter. When we hike in the white cedar forest on Cape Cod, we watch for ticks as much as we watch for butterflies. I want them to know this bit of nature before it is gone, for what would we lose in a world without the sound of bumblebees, where we may never be startled by the shadow of a giant moth or be amazed by the alien life in our own front yards?

H.L.M. LEE is an electronics engineer with a background in English literature. While owning and operating a small high-tech company, he also writes web content and marketing materials, and develops video scripts for a scientific journal. He has recently finished a novel, *Bleeding in Babylon*, about the Iraq War. Additional information about him and his writing may be found on his web site at www.HLMLee.com.

Autumn Waking

by Dana Colecchia Getz

A steaming mug of tea presses hot into my palms, warming the ache of fall. Looking out into the backyard, I watch the leaves rain down with a soft "shhh" as if the universe is urging me to quiet and pay attention.

I rarely have time these days to pause and step outside of the rush that is middle age—this middle place that's filled with children and parents, mortgages and mammograms. But when I do, I realize that more often than not I feel a bit like that tree behind the porch clinging to a few determined green leaves, but otherwise exposed.

When I was younger, spring was my favorite season. The green hope of it all buoyed me out of my winter funk and into a manic joy that extended for months. But now that I'm older I relish these early mornings of hot tea and wool socks—days that lull me in slow blinks until fully awake and alive. The trees that I once viewed as bare and depressing now grasp my admiration in their spare determination. They are exposed but rooted, raw and regal.

I was once soft dewy grass and subtle knolls of dandelions. I look in the mirror and see today that at 40 I am more angular and pitched. My eyes are not so bright, but discerning. My cheeks are not so full, but lined with remnants of joy. My forehead is a testament to hours at night awake and fretting over children who will not sleep and in-laws who are sick. Stripped bare of youth, I remain solid and steady.

The bright green of spring is still a blessing, but now I notice and respect the dedicated roots and the rough, winding bark that remains behind, weathered and prepping for winter.

DANA COLECCHIA GETZ is a Pittsburgh-based writer, traveler and entrepreneur. Her work has appeared in *The Christian Science Monitor*, *Go World Travel*, and *Mamalode*.

Seeing Beyond Our Scars

by Melissa Hart

At first glance, I didn't notice John Wesley Powell's missing arm. In the black and white photos that appear on Utah's historical signage, the Civil War veteran and Western explorer appears so engaged by whatever landscape he and the Paiute Headman Tau-Gu gaze at that his vacant right sleeve faded into the background—irrelevant in the face of appreciation for the wilderness.

"A mine ball hit his arm at the Battle of Shiloh." I recounted his story for my husband Jonathan on a family trip to Zion National Park.

Powell survived and crossed the country to become the first Anglo explorer on the Colorado and Green Rivers. In his journal, he describes plummeting over a cliff and hanging by his only hand until a quick-thinking friend shed his long johns and dangled them over the mountainside.

"The friend pulled Powell to safety," I reported and then fell silent, contemplating the moment of faith that must have informed the man's decision to let go of whatever bush or boulder he clung to in order to snatch at woolen salvation.

My jacket sleeve had hiked up while I drove; a scar like a frigid river snaked from wrist to elbow. My tongue ached where surgeons five months before had excised a cancerous lesion and replaced it with tissue and muscle from my arm. Pain ricocheted from the skin graft three inches square whenever I bumped it, or my six-year old daughter reached to hold my hand. We'd planned this trip to Zion before I ever knew I'd have to have the six-hour surgery, before I'd been maimed.

I discovered the tumor on a camping trip at Oregon's Waldo Lake while paddling a kayak and eating a Clif bar. When doctors told me the painful spot on my tongue would have to be removed, necessitating the surgery and a graft, I wept for my lost luck—43 years of disease-free, mostly injury-free, adventure.

"I'll never hike again!" I wailed to Jonathan in a bare, sterile room the antithesis of the mountains and coastal trails we usually frequented. "I'm condemned to live the rest of my life on the couch."

But cancer, it turns out, isn't always a death sentence—especially in the form of a Stage I tumor on a healthy woman's tongue. A few weeks after surgery, I could stagger through Douglas firs in Eugene's Buford Park wilderness and step over banana slugs and rough-skinned newts, newly appreciative of their small lives. But I couldn't talk clearly, and I hurt ... all the time.

To ensure that the cancer hadn't spread, surgeons had taken a dime-sized piece of my tongue and 23 lymph nodes from my neck. My surgery sites swelled and throbbed with any aerobic exercise; after a two-mile run, I lurched through the back door dizzy with pain, lisping to Jonathan, "I'm thcared I'll path out."

I buried my running shoes and swimsuit in the closet, hid my bike helmet and kayak paddle in the back of the shed, and prayed for recovery. I could hike, yes, but alone unless friends and family wanted to ramble along rivers and over hills in silence. I canceled adventures planned in my pre-surgery state—a snowshoeing weekend, a day of kayaking, camping with friends.

"Should we postpone our trip to Zion?" I wondered the night before our flight.

"Why?" Jonathan demanded.

Decades ago, he'd broken his back. Now, he looked up from packing his duffel bag. "I climbed a hundred and fifty-four steps from a boat to an island off the coast of California in a body cast and hiked all over. Pack your pain meds—you'll be fine."

And initially, I *was* fine. Zion is an intoxicating distraction from discomfort. With Muir's "Come to the mountains and get their good tidings" on repeat in my head, I followed Jonathan and our daughter past sandstone caves and up to Emerald Pool to look for frogs. We climbed the Archeology Trail and examined boulders, wondering about the Paiute who'd lived and cooked there. We walked up to Weeping Rock and my child caught water drops on her tongue. "Stick out *your* tongue, Mommy," she said.

"I can't." I stared out at the lovely canyon and gritted my teeth against pain.

The previous summer, I'd trekked through Oregon's Three Sisters Wilderness with a 35-pound pack. Now, my neck and tongue muscles ached from a backpack filled with nothing but a water bottle and an apple inside. My left arm hung limp—the leopard-print vet wrap I insisted on wearing over the graft site kept slipping up to reveal the shiny scar below my jacket sleeve, as heart-breaking as the scrawled graffiti on a fallen tree near the trailhead.

Jonathan peered at me and put aside his camera. "Need to go back to the hotel?"

A hotel, when I'd longed to camp.

In the setting sun, my daughter stopped to examine a beetle. She shed her silk long johns and stuffed them in my pack. I thought of John Wesley Powell, of his empty sleeve and his resiliency. "There's another hour of light." I forced enthusiasm into my voice. "Let's hike the Pa'rus Trail."

Pa'rus is more of a path, really, paved and open to cyclists and leashed dogs. It winds through sagebrush and wildflowers, from the Human Museum to Zion's Visitor Center, flanked by towering red and orange cliffs. I lagged behind my family, listening to them chatter about insects and vultures. Looking up hurt my neck. Talking hurt my tongue. Despite my stunning surroundings, my optimism began to erode. I hadn't smoked a cigarette ever. I'd sipped a glass of red wine with some dinners, but that was all. I'd exercised every day of my life. My doctor suspected I'd contracted the tumor from some bizarre virus.

I'm scarred for life. Self-pity slowed my steps, settled upon me dark as the deepening shadows cast by Zion's rocky spires.

Surely, Powell, upon first contemplating his missing limb, slipped into despair. Lucky is the person who can surface from disaster to find salvation in the world outside what the Buddhists call the "small sense of self." But the world outside beckons and heals.

As I plodded on, two cyclists sped by me and stopped at a sign. I approached reluctantly, letting my husband and daughter do the bulk of the socializing. "Nice evening for a bicycle ride," I lisped and fell silent, mortified.

The woman took off her bike helmet and shook back her gray hair, gazing around her with wide eyes. "Isn't it gorgeous?" She laughed with pleasure. When she turned, I saw that she sported a giant black hairy growth, maybe a mole, on one side of her face. "Enjoy your evening!" She waved and rode on.

A few minutes later, we met a twenty-something couple with their Australian shepherd. The dog bounded toward us to snuffle our hands.

"Mommy!" My daughter tugged my sleeve. "Why does that dog have three legs?"

I winced and stayed silent, unwilling to lisp in front of the vibrant young couple.

"Hit by a car," the man explained. "Vet had to amputate."

"Off leash, she runs faster than we do." The woman strained to hold the dog back. "Have a nice walk—we gotta go!"

In myths and fairy tales, life-changing meetings often happen in threes. Still, I stared in mild shock five minutes later at the smiling sunburned man who pushed a young woman in a wheelchair along the path. From her stiff limbs and twisted neck, I guessed severe cerebral palsy. The man stopped when he saw us and handed Jon his binoculars. "That's the largest natural arch around." He pointed up at a reddish stone curvature across part of the mountaintop, barely perceptible to our eyes.

My child, endlessly curious, pointed at the woman in the wheelchair. "Is she your wife or your daughter?"

"I'm out camping with my three kids," he replied. "She's my oldest."

The woman's head lolled, and her mouth stretched into a smile. Her father handed me the binoculars. "How odd." I peered at the arch, there in front of us the whole time, but we couldn't see it until he showed us.

Self-pity gave way to appreciation for the metaphor. So many of us have scars, some as prominent as the one on my arm, the ones jutting across my husband's back. If we're wise, we move past trauma to see what we still have ... so much sky, so much water, so many trees and stars and boulders. The wisest of us, like the man standing in front of me now, allow adversity to deepen gratitude for what we've been given and share it with others.

Pulled to safety, I knelt beside the woman in the wheelchair. "Are you having a good vacation?"

I kept talking, though the woman's eyes looked elsewhere. "Zion is the most beautiful park I've ever seen."

I lifted her father's binoculars to my eyes and my sleeve rode up once more as I focused on that newly-revealed arch. I shrugged off my jacket and let it fall to the ground, rejoicing in the evening sun's warmth upon my bare arms.

MELISSA HART is contributing editor at *The Writer Magazine*, and her essays have appeared in *Orion, High Country News, The Washington Post, The Chicago Tribune, The Los Angeles Times, The Advocate, The Chronicle of Higher Education, Hemispheres*, and numerous other publications. She is the author of two adult memoirs—*Gringa: A Contradictory Girlhood* (Seal, 2009) and *Wild Within: How Rescuing Owls Inspired a Family* (Lyons, 2015)—and a YA novel, *Avenging the Owl* (Sky Pony, 2016). Please feel free to view published clips at www.melissahart.com.

Swimming

by Sheri McGregor

We walk up the rocky, rutted path. My footsteps are light and carefree. My young adult son's steps are more careful, a little off rhythm, but solid. The rod beneath his skin is invisible. Few detect his tiny limp, I realize. Or notice the fraction of an inch of compensation, "microscopic" he calls it, that keeps him on his feet.

"Look, a frog." He bends, cups his hand around a spotted gray frog the size of a nickel. He stands and motions toward the pond, about a half mile away—little more than a dark, glassy dot from this distance. "The little guy's going the wrong way." He opens his hand a little. The tiny frog peeks out, bulging eyes almost as big as its body. My son closes the gap between his fingers. "I'll take him back where he belongs."

The sun is bright, the day before us free and happy, but my mind goes back to winter a year ago. To the ICU room swathed in darkness, the folds of light from the nurse's desk beyond the glass wall pushing beneath the curtain. They didn't like his door closed, but in those few lucid moments when his pain became unbearable between morphine doses, my son wanted privacy, as if blotting out the sounds of intercom calls and other patients' beeping machinery could blot out the sudden turn of events that had changed his life. He'd suffered the constant indignity of lying in a flimsy gown, being poked and prodded by intruding hospital personnel. Tubes jutted from nearly every natural orifice and a few manmade. As his mother, rendered helpless of a way to comfort my barely adult son, going against their rules to slide shut the glass door was a wafer-thin sliver of control, something I could do when there was little else.

We walk along. Him with the frog, me holding the leash as the dog, a yellow Lab, trots between us. Her pink tongue lolls. There is new growth all around, this year's cleansing, record-breaking rains completing a pattern of rebirth that began with last season's wildfires. I'm reminded of getting outdoors last spring. As color emerged in my son's cheeks, emaciated from a slow recovery when he couldn't eat, charred oak trees budded. Pale green leaves sprouted green wreaths at the base of their trunks. Flowers that hadn't bloomed in years uncurled in profusion, stretching from the ashen earth to meet the sunlight. During that time, my son took tiny steps away from home, away from my care, regaining his tremulous stride into adult independence that a drunk driver without a license had stolen from him.

By the end of summer, with pain still his constant companion, he had grown well enough to return to college. He didn't want to, which led to a careful dance of push and pull.

"You don't realize how fast the time will go," I'd say. "Take this opportunity, please."

It was one I never had. My parents didn't offer the choice to stay home and go to school. When I finally went to college decades later, my life was complex, studying yet another ball to juggle.

"I'm young," he'd tell me. "There's lots of time."

In October, he moved out. As he rode off in a friend's car stuffed with his things, I cried. The days of his extended hospitalization, the knowledge that life is a precarious tightrope each of us walks, were etched in after his senseless, near-death crash. But he needed to find his way.

That we're hiking together now a year later, trudging up the path in health, is a miracle. I look over, notice his slight limp, and realize again that no one else sees it. His scars have also faded, narrow pink lines on his legs, his arms, and across his abdomen indicating trauma, but not doing justice to his suffering.

We stop above the pond, the sunlight glinting off its surface. A desk full of work awaits me, but there's time for that later. Now it's time to stop. The wind carries the pungent scent of free-growing sage that lines the surrounding hills and grows in thick clusters near the pond. The day is perfect.

My grown-up son takes a final look at the tiny frog nestled in his palm, then carries it to safety. At the water's edge, he crouches and opens his hand. The frog hops into the air, an arc of movement that ends with an insignificant splash. "There he goes." His grin brings a glimpse of boyhood to his dimpled adult face. "He'll be fine. He's swimming now."

I smile, happy, touched by my son's sweet nature. Images of his tenderness with pets, memories of his people-person words spoken at just the right moment, and years of his mischievous charm, flood my heart and mind. Once, when I was having a bad day, I told him I felt awful. He looked at me with a glint in his eye. "You sure are," he said. "To see you, everyone is full of awe."

During the final leg of the hike, my son tells me some secrets; dreams and aspirations he's beginning to plan. "Not quite yet," he says, "but soon. All of my friends will be shocked, but now you won't be surprised." He grins. "I haven't told a soul until now, Mom. It's not something to blab around."

"I won't tell anyone," I say, committing to silence.

Later, as he drives away from the house, the familiar urge to cry unfurls, a ribbon of pride and joy and sadness blooming deep in my throat. I smile and wave. Turning to go back inside, I notice a tiny clump of mint in the space between the walkway steps. It's escaped from my garden bed. I stoop and pinch off a leaf, sniff the soft, sweet scent.

Near the road, my son pulls shut the big wrought iron gate. He waves, and I watch him drive away. The engine's roar fades into the distance, melds into the world beyond our home, beyond his mother's palm, and the gate that once cupped him in safety.

I turn to go inside. He's fine, I think. *He's swimming now.*

SHERI MCGREGOR's essays and articles have appeared in a variety of publications both in the U.S. and internationally. Nonfiction books include her three popular hiking guides for the San Diego area. Her first self-help book, *Done With The Crying: Help and Healing for Mothers of Estranged Adult Children* (Sowing Creek Press, 2016) helps hurting parents around the world.

A Place Called Tséyi'

by Leeanna T. Torres

Ron's pack of cigarettes sits inside the cup holder of the car's center console. He coughs as we drive west, and I wonder how long he's been a smoker—years, decades, a lifetime? I do not ask. Instead I watch the rain in the distance, falling miles and miles away. The Great American West allows for this sort of view, the kind that stretches on for miles, for lifetimes. I think of the Rain Spirits, imagine them dressed in timid and canvas, unrecognizable to those who do not know them. Then it all takes hold—the blue and the greyness of sky, the weightlessness of clouds that bring us water, the way Ron grips the wheel of the car with both hands, the smell of cigarettes never leaving him, driving north, closer to Arizona than we were an hour ago. This becomes the vessel of today's sobriety, my sobriety. I grow sleepy and realize suddenly that it has been years since I have hiked up a *mesa*.

We travel on to Tséyi'.

In Gallup we stop at a gas station. I head inside to use the restroom while Ron remains outside, his large Santa-Claus belly leaning into the trunk as he settles himself into a stance. He lights up and pulls on the cigarette with a breath that seems urgent rather than enjoyable. We are deep in the heart of Navajo country now. Big sky country. Land of the Diné. Land where legends of the West were made. As I exit the gas station, a candy bar in hand, I see Ron still smoking, lingering in his habit the way I linger in sentiment under the big blue sky. We are co-workers, Ron and I, and even in this ordinary travel I sense the largeness of where we are traveling.

Sacred. Place. And cigarettes.

On the road from Gallup to Chinle the *llanos* are green. Monsoon rain has been falling. But instead of finding calm among the green of late summer in the southwest, resentment and fear grow, thoughts of Tío Johnny in the hospital—dying—and my own mother, also battling that demon called cancer, caught in that space between remission and treatment. Traveling to Tséyi' and I am plagued by thoughts of sickness and suffering. Mortality. Ron drives on, unaware of my discontent. I smile as I sit in the passenger seat, keeping private matters private, searching for solace in our travels towards the sacred. Tséyi'.

We travel by car, guided by map and speed limit signs, while all around us the clouds gather onto themselves. We approach the state line, crossing over into Arizona. The radio picks up an oldies station. Outside of Window Rock, Arizona, the car climbs up into the juniper tree line, then ponderosa pine. Soon the highway is only a two-lane, and we follow behind a grey Ford single-cab truck with a "rez dog" riding in the back bed.

"Rediscover the heart of the Navajo Nation," reads the website of the official National Park Service page, "For nearly 5,000 years, people have lived in these canyons - longer than anyone has lived uninterrupted anywhere on the Colorado Plateau... Navajo families continue to make their homes, raise livestock, and farm the lands in these canyons." And I cling to words as much as I cling to places of power, in hopes that they will change me in ways I cannot change myself.

Traveling, I am a contradiction, a visitor, a passer-by. While I am a daughter of the American Southwest, I am not of *this* place. This place is something else, a place of different spirts, different ghosts, different winds. I cannot fix my own anger, my own disappointments, my own deeply hidden fears. So I travel. I seek out places of power.

Tséyi' is more commonly known as Canyon de Chelly. While it is officially a National Park, it is more importantly still a living and sacred place to and for "The People," the Diné, more commonly known as the Navajo.

Ron steers the car onto one of the official "overlooks" of the canyon's north rim and pulls into the parking lot slowly. I rush to open the door even before he's turned off the engine, and I hurry towards the lookout ledge, eager and urgent. Ron sluggishly gets out of the car and lights up, more eager for the cigarette than for the canyon. Ron's been here before. This place is not new or exciting for his tired eyes. But he is patient and brings me to this place just the same. He's played this game of tour-guide before.

Standing at the overlook, I see the river winding far below, a thousand feet down. Sun is beginning to set. This is a place of water and time. A place of rock and wind. To stand before a place so large is to become and remain inherently small. Standing at the edge of the canyon, history and legend and geology bow to the sky which endures forever, rain in the distance, thunder on the heels of dark and distant clouds.

The sun is setting. Ron's stance behind me indicates he's eager to leave. I take no photos of the canyon. I leave with the image of its grandeur in my memory alone. Something about the way the breeze rushes across the rock tells me not to snap a photo, not to disturb the moment with a flash and something kept. Ron puts out his cigarette. Deep thunder sounds as he exhales the last of his smoke before reaching for the car door.

What is this movement we make from ordinary to sacred, from casual to powerful, from oblivious to a state of deep and intended gratitude? I ask too much of this place, this space, this time.

That night we have dinner at the hotel restaurant. Both Ron and I order the Chicken-Fried-Steak-Special as described on the whiteboard near the door; the words drawn in green marker. I pick at the mashed potatoes on my plate, envisioning the scene of rock and pine from an overlook sectioned safely by metal piping. I sit at the dinner table making small conversation with Ron, while in the back of my mind I remain at the canyon, still and unspeaking, lingering in the place called Tséyi', canyon of myth, power, spirit.

I do not find illuminating peace. Tomorrow we'll attend our business meeting at the Many Farms Chapter, shaking hands and speaking opportunity, and then we will leave. What will have changed? Will I return the same as when I left? I look to places to heal me, to change my mind, to change my heart, to lessen the load of resentment and fear. I look to Tséyi' for revelation, for healing. I look to take, to receive, to be given. But what the canyon offers is quite the opposite.

I do not find illuminating peace. Rather, I find a stance of momentary acceptance.

Tío Johnny will die. My mother will continue to suffer. And my only job is to be present for them, if only in the small space and place we call love, at a distance, helpless to help them, hopeful to just be present. Sobriety teaches me about powerlessness, but it is Tséyi' that reveals a stance which is simply existing in the moment, without want, without expectations, without resolution or blessing. I do not find peace, rather, what is given is more than peace. It is a stillness. An unspeaking. A prayer of remaining.

Sometimes I struggle in sobriety, and I struggle in the face of family mortality, feeling one shake the other. But I return to Tséyi'. Again and again, I return to the memory, the lingering, of Tséyi'. Red rock canyon of myth, home of the Diné. I do not leave as a sentimental tourist, nor a romantic wannabe. I am always at the canyon edge, small and aware of the unspeakable wild before me.

We experience "sacred places" as only tourists sometimes, as passersby, and we want what we want, and we take what we take, and we remember what we remember. But always, the place itself remains, and the sacred we cannot take with us, like a token, like a souvenir. The sacred remains, untouched by our wanting hearts, remains where it has always been, where it will continue to exist. So, I leave Tséyi' without taking a photo, without buying a postcard. I leave with the rain, an unspoken stance, and Ron is the driver yet again, taking us back across the border and toward home again.

But there is a beckoning; I sense it traveling through the distance of this great expanse, relentless yet not wanting. And I understand for a moment that we belong to this world, death and joy alike, suffering and sobriety and everything in between. And while Ron's breath pulls hard on his cigarettes, my own hand tugs on the wrapper of a chocolate bar, and in the parking lot of a railroad town we embrace our small addictions as casually as the sky embraces breeze. Ron is smoking, the white stick of tobacco lingering between his fingers, an unconventional prayer, so delicate, so momentary, and his breath pulls in, in, in. To take it all in, to remain, and then to exhale. The sound of the busy interstate beside us, the vast expanse of a western sky reminding me of today, only today.

LEEANNA T. TORRES is a native daughter of the American Southwest, with deep cultural Indo-Hispanic roots in New Mexico. She has spent the last 15 years as an environmental professional working throughout the West. Her essays have been published in *The New Mexico Review*, *Tupelo (Press) Quarterly*, and *Blue Mesa Review*. Essays are also forthcoming in *Eastern Iowa Review* and the upcoming anthology, *Waves: A Confluence of Women's Voices* (AROHO Foundation).

Finding My Bearings with Men

by Eva Schlesinger

"Hey Bear, coming through." Our guide, Dan, spoke in a low tone. My hip waders squelched through mud, past grasses that came up over my knees, into the lush green meadow. Grizzlies grazed, chewing sedge. A male bear's head rested on his mate's back. Another male loped by, gazing with oval, brown eyes. Males, both bears and humans, surrounded me on Alaska's Katmai Coast.

In Katmai, southwest of Anchorage, humans haven't hunted bears in decades, so bears don't feel threatened by them. My small boat tour offered close views of bears and other wildlife. I wanted to get up close to the grizzly bears. I wasn't so sure, however, about a group of men.

Growing up, I felt silenced by boys. When I said no, boys, and later men, challenged me, their desires dominating mine. Now I felt shy and tentative in a group of males. Human males, that is. Surrounded by grizzlies, I felt safe and happy. Animals make me feel whole and content, like they're a part of my family.

Every day we took a skiff to shore. I was the lone female with three others (another guest, Manuel; Dan; and Captain Jesse), walking on narrow trails made by bears, watching a sow and her cubs drink from a stream. A brown cub twirled a white stick like a baton, tossing it into the air. Another cub stood on its hind legs, checking us out. Bears dug for clams, leaving nickel-sized tooth marks in shells.

When our guide suggested we visit a different area of the meadow, Manuel said, "Is this okay with you, Eva?"

Back on the boat, when the predominantly male crew decided things about our activities, he asked, "Would you like to do this, too?"

Usually, I nodded. Sometimes, I said no.

During evening discussions of bear behavior, the deep tones drowned out my squeaky one. Captain Jesse threw me a life preserver when he turned his head of scraggly black curls to mine. "What would you like to say, Eva?"

One night, perched on a high chair in the wheelhouse, I kept my eyes on the orcas and otters swimming as the boat moved from Hallo to Kukak Bay. Captain Jesse showed me on the map where we had been and were going.

I thought of where I had been—scared to trust men—and where I was headed, through uncharted territory, guided by my own radar. I asked a question, and instead of laughing the way men previously have, he said, "Splendid question. You have an excellent way of phrasing things."

On our last day, rain soaked my hat, splashing like tears across my glasses. Captain Jesse presented his hand to me as I wobbled on pointy, gray stones, slippery with rockweed. Examining crusty barnacles, our group huddled around a jellyfish that looked like four white ferns intersecting under glass. The ferns appeared to be at a crossroads.

Or I was.

As I glanced around, lamenting that we hadn't yet seen any bears that morning, my eyes fell on the others. Warmth eddied through me. I felt kinship with them.

In my search to find the bears, I had found new friends. I had found care and kindness. And whether I said, "Yes, I want to do this," or I said, "No, I do not," I had felt heard and respected by a group of men.

EVA SCHLESINGER is a contributor to Chicken Soup's *Thanks To My Mom* (2015) and *Tough Times, Tough People* (2009), and is the author of four poetry chapbooks. When not writing, she photographs wildlife and draws wildly colorful, whimsical animals. She has biked and hiked the Bay Area for more than 20 years.

Solace from a Sleeping Volcano

by Jean O'Neill

I want to go back to that lake in Tacoma, the one just beyond the woods where I watched fireworks on the Fourth of July and squealed when the mucky sand squished in my toes. At sunset, I could see Mount Rainier, the sleeping volcano surrounded by yellow and pink. Across the brown and lapping lake, I had watched this mountain under its blanket of snow, imagined its eyes closed and the lava inside keeping it warm and cozy. Don't wake it up; don't make it angry.

I want to go back to Mount Rainier where the sky was so thick with blue it looked purple, almost like midnight. I was maybe five years old the day we all climbed in the snow, up the side of the mountain, in only our sneakers and gloveless hands. My family with our Army base neighbors had all driven out from the base in Fort Lewis to climb up and wander through the mountain's trails. I had called it a mountain, not knowing what really lay beneath the snowy blanket. I loved how this particular mountain had a divot at the top instead of a peak.

"It's not a mountain!" my sister insisted. "It's a sleeping volcano."

I was afraid we'd make it angry. "What if it wakes up when we're on it?" I was assured that the volcano was not likely to wake up and erupt.

We followed my father into the woods on the hard-packed snow, while people on skis sloshed and shushed down the groomed mountainside. I wore a heavy wool sweater the color of a fresh bruise that matched the sky. We hiked the snowy, sloping trail that wound through the woods. Out of breath and out of energy, hands cold and stinging, we stopped for a break somewhere in the middle. The fat and tall pine trees poked at the purple sky, and Janet took off her coat. She wore only a short-sleeved t-shirt underneath.

"You're gonna get in trouble!" I warned. How could she take off her coat with all this cold snow around her? We both came from military families; we followed rules and orders. When it was cold outside, we wore sweaters and coats. These were the rules.

"I'm too hot," she replied. I pushed my own sleeves up to my elbows while the bright white snow burned my eyes. A picture of us shows Janet in her tiny shirt sleeves and me in my heavy wool sweater. She's already more than a foot taller than me but she's not even a year older. I'd always been small for my age; "little" was a word my mother often used to describe me. "Jean, squeeze back in the corner; you're little."

On the way home, I sat in the middle of the bench seat in the back of the car, smushed between my brother and sister with my feet on the hump. I looked out the back window of our little green Pacer and watched the midnight sky fade to light blue, watched the sleeping volcano get smaller and smaller, and then for a while, I probably slept, too.

I want to go back to the summer I turned five, to the Officer's Club Beach near Tacoma where I pretended to swim. I held myself up in the shallow water with one arm, then pretended to stroke while I switched hands. My father asked if I wanted to swim, and I said, "Yes! Look, I can swim!" But it wasn't swimming at all.

My dad was a Captain in the Army but I never saw him in a uniform. He wore khakis and casual slacks and button-down shirts with the sleeves rolled up to his forearms. They were muscular and hairy, manly, fatherly arms. On his right hand he wore a large ring from Manhattan College where he had earned a degree in Engineering. He didn't drive trains, so I didn't understand what this meant. He wore a silver watch that clasped around his thick wrist and when he took it off, I would play with it, wear it like a bracelet. It was heavy on my wrist and I had to push it all the way up to my elbow to make it fit. My father's palms were soft, the knuckles cracked and dry. He smoked Kool cigarettes and often smelled of smoke and stale beer, a smell I would later always associate with him, but one I never noticed as a child. Between him and my mother, we were always surrounded by a cloud of smoke, shrouded by a blanket of happy ignorance.

He scooped me up from where I waded in three inches of water, took enough steps to be waist high and tossed me into the Pacific Ocean. I flew through the air, splashed into the ocean, kicked and flapped my way to the surface. I could see the sleeping volcano floating on top of the water far away in the distance. It appeared as though I could swim to it, just swim across the ocean and touch it.

After that day, I didn't hang around in three inches of water; I didn't have to pretend to anymore. My sister no longer needed to piggy-back me to the diving dock at the Officer's Club Beach. I could now swim there myself. And as always, the sleeping volcano hung in the sky, as if watching and waiting like a cautious grandparent.

I want to go back to our garage door in Olympia where my brother would take me for rides. He would lift the garage door and tell me to hang on, and I'd dangle from the bottom of the door. And then he'd jump up and pull it back down. We'd ride down and then we'd jump off.

"Again!" I'd shout. It was like floating or flying or both. I want to go back to that time when I had a big brother who looked after me, who called me his little sister, and made sure I had fun. Back then, family was permanent, and blood determined a closeness that would never be questioned. Two years later, my brother would blame himself for our father's death. As a twelve-year-old boy, he'd tell my father to drop dead, and the next day, my father would die in a car accident. Thirty years later, he'd blame me for killing our mother. I had caused all of her stress, and that's why she died, he'd say. Then, he'd claim that I was useless and disposable, and never speak to me again. As I rode the garage door, that hazy and distant sleeping volcano hovering somewhere in the afternoon sky, I didn't know that a brother's love wouldn't always be unconditional.

The year I turned five, a two-wheeler with big U-shaped handlebars and a black banana seat appeared on my birthday. The chain guard was painted in a colorful carnival scene, and the bike itself was like the sky on a bright, sunny day.

My dad stood with me in the street, my sister by his side. She and my father held the new bike while I climbed on. My sister watched from behind as my father coached me. I held the handlebars and put my feet on the pedals. My head was down, facing the front tire.

"What are you looking at?" he asked.

"The tire." I said. "That's what Renee told me to do." Renee, a third-grader in my brother's class had tried to teach me how to ride a bike earlier that summer.

"Hold onto the handlebars," Renee had said, "And pedal your feet. Look at the tire in front of you." She had hair called "dirty blonde" and I wondered if that meant it would be "yellow blonde" if she washed it. She and my sister held the bike up for me as I pedaled. I didn't so much pedal as let the pedals move my feet. I didn't know to put pressure down, and as my sister and Renee moved the bike along, the pedals moved on their own.

"I won't let go," my sister had said. But the bike was too heavy for her seven-year-old frame to hold, and I had no sense of balance. We didn't get very far.

But now with my dad teaching me, I had to unlearn what Renee had said.

"No, no," my father said. "Keep your head up and look at the road in front of you."

"Then how will I know where the bike will go?"

"It will go where you're looking," he said. I started to pedal, and he promised not to let go. I pedaled and pedaled until I heard my sister shout, "She's doing it! She's doing it!" I turned my head over my shoulder and saw my sister jump up and down. Then the bike and I crashed in the street. She ran to me and made me get back on. Many years later, my sister's 20-year marriage would crash, and our roles would reverse.

That day in Olympia when I learned how to ride a bike with my sister, my father stood in the street and grinned, proud of us both. Behind him I could still see Mount Rainier, tiny and faint like a painting or a dream or the moon watching over me in the distance. My father watched his two daughters struggle together, the older one holding the younger one up and running behind, and then suddenly the younger one pedaling away.

I want to go back to that time when pain was just physical, when I could dust myself off and get back on again. My memories take me back to that time when hearts didn't hurt, when family was less complicated, when trust was never a question. In my mind, I can go back to that time when problems were so far ahead of me they didn't really exist, when possibilities were as endless and as simple as dreaming them up. In my mind, I can go back to that time when the sight of a sleeping volcano could calm and soothe and promise to always remain constant.

JEAN O'NEILL earned her MFA in Creative Writing from Chatham University in Pittsburgh, PA and is an editor at *Bloodletters Literary Magazine - A Space for Healing*. Her work has appeared online and in print in *The Rusty Nail* and *Fringe Magazine*. Jean finds her home in Pittsburgh with her very large and deaf cat named MarshMellow.

My Friend Carl

by Camille Armantrout

Carl lives on a wooded promontory with a view of the flood plain. Mainstay in an ever-changing world, he's been standing tall for decades. Yesterday I walked the half mile through the woods to spend time with Carl. I went in the morning before it was hot, armed with a spider stick, and prepared to retreat if accosted by too many black gnats and mosquitoes. But summer storms have reduced the spider webs to bearable, and mosquitoes and gnats were also at a minimum.

My legs are strong and sure on this familiar trail. I hit my stride about five minutes out. I'm drenched in living earth, fragrant with pine needles and leaf mulch. Generations of trees surround me, from tiny sprouts to giant sentinels. The air hums with woodpeckers and cicadas. I swing my head to the left when a squirrel rustles in the undergrowth. Sometimes deer startle me, leaping up and blasting away like gunshots. Once I came across a fox, sitting in the middle of the path to scratch at fleas. Another time, a Barred Owl swooped down to take a better look, then flew back to its perch to keep an eye on me.

Carl receives me in his reassuringly taciturn way, eyes forward. He reaches out with solid, steady limbs and I feel safe. Without a word, Carl and I are in our happy place once again. He is a beautiful example of his species, an American Beech. Or perhaps he is, as I often joke, a son of a beech. Nature gave Carl markings that resemble a human face on the side facing the stream. He has a jaunty mustache with a twig sprouting from the corner, like a pipe stem or cigarette. This year a praying mantis chose to build an egg case on his cigarette.

Old forest lore referred to the majestic beech as queen of the forest. Their trunks are smooth and straight, mottled with white and gray spots. They have the peculiarity of retaining their leaves all winter, only losing them when new growth pushes them out. Their leaves provide a spark of ocher in the cold, monochromatic months. Surely this tenacity is one of the things that appeals to me as I walk towards the winter of my life.

The neighbors pooled their resources to install a cedar bench beside Carl for my sixty-second birthday. Jason built the bench, leaving the legs an extra two feet long. Lyle and fourteen-year-old Amie loaded it into the tractor bucket and drove it into the woods, carrying the heavy thing between them the last fifty feet. Doug and Jason made four holes and sunk the legs into the earth. The bench is sturdy and wide, and smells like my mother's cedar hope chest.

I climb on and sit, legs dangling. The size of Carl's bench turns me into a youngster. I lay back and peer up through the understory at the sky. My heart swells and my eyes get moist. Time stops. I'm alone, and connected. There is only this moment, and this place, and yet I'm aware of all the moments of my life. All the good ones, anyway.

I think about my friends who cared enough to add this bench to my favorite spot. I recall our many shared meals, the birthday candles and wishes, and remember delicious Sunday dinners at my Nana's when I was a little girl. My thoughts wander forward to our daughter Emily's upcoming wedding, and what will be our first glimpse of her new baby boy. I think about my husband, Bob, and how lucky I am to have a partner who gets my twisted sense of humor; and how relieved we both are that he is well and recovering his smile after a bout of Bell's Palsy.

I caught part of the "TED Radio Hour" the other day. They were talking about aging and time. As we age, they said, we become more positive, yet joyful occasions often bring a tear to our eye. We find ourselves experiencing the past, present, and future simultaneously. Surely holding our grandson for the first time will trigger a montage of feelings; all the way back to Emily as a tiny girl, and fast forwarding to imagine little Nolan as a grown man.

This is why I visit Carl in his special place. To think, remember, imagine, let go, connect, rejoice, and weep. Carl seems to understand. He never questions. He just stands there with his cigarette and looks off across the ages.

CAMILLE ARMANTROUT writes from North Carolina where she lives with her husband, Bob, in a wooded neighborhood of friends. She has written about their travels to Africa in the book, *Two Brauds Abroad: A Departure from Life as We Know It*, which she co-authored with Stephanie De La Garza. Her work has been published in *Once Upon An Expat: An Anthology*. Her pursuits include cooking, gardening, yoga, and long walks. Find out more about Camille at her Plastic Farm Animals blog: www.troutsfarm.com/PFA.

Murmuration

by Sidney Stevens

I'm not sure when I noticed I was in a parade. A parade of one.

It seemed my spectators arrived at once. One moment the oaks, maples and elms lining the trail were bare against the brilliant late-fall sky, limbs and branches twisting upward like reaching arms. The next minute the treetops were filled with iridescent, vibrating black bodies.

Hundreds, maybe thousands of starlings, on mass migration, draped over me like a noisy, living canopy. Spectators to my parade. Or so it seemed. But why?

Parades show off something beautiful, celebrate victories, commemorate holidays and anniversaries. But they also march criminals through streets and ne'er-do-wells out of town.

My parade felt more like that. Did this crowd sense my numbness? Had they gathered to witness my uncertainty? I stood for a moment, letting the thunderous cacophony roll over me.

I'd traveled this trail almost daily for years, wandering through the quiet forests, past farm fields and ravines. These places brought me peace. But lately I'd lost my way. I kept waiting for inspiration and revival that used to come from moments among growing things, when my mind could slow down. But this place where I did my best thinking, the refuge where I worked out the knots of my life, had lost its ability to stir and energize me.

The pungent forest air wafted over me day after day, clear sky or clouds sprawled overhead, sunlight dappled the trail floor or rain dropped. But my sanctuary no longer brought answers or release. My life felt stagnant.

This was my parade of shame. The giant pulsating chorus above me seemed abuzz with cat-calls. Countless beady eyes gawked with scorn. Or so it seemed.

You come to certain plateaus in life, where you need to grow, or you won't anymore. I'd seen it happen to others, and I was there. I could feel the fear and inertia, a block of doubts about trying something new with my writing, my artwork, my life. I was successful enough as a freelance writer, had published some essays and even tried a novel once, but it never got published. I didn't try again.

I'd recently begun dabbling in mosaic-making. I was doing work that others seemed to like, but ... but what? My creations usually pleased me. I pushed myself to excel, but something left me unfulfilled, even when I thought I was giving my all.

I shivered in the sunlight and trudged on, head down, feeling suddenly exposed, as though my dark-winged witnesses could see the stuck places inside me, the restlessness that worked at cross purposes, the unfair twist of mind that ever nagged and haunted me with a sense that I was meant to do more.

I glanced up from the litter of ocher leaves on the trail. Something odd was taking shape overhead. Maybe a trick of imagination, but as I moved my audience seemed to move with me. Improbably, batches of starlings directly above me opened their wings and glided to trees further down, hopscotching from branch to branch as I paraded beneath them.

This was beyond my control, this mass of starlings. Predatory. Aware. Would they swoop with eagle talons to carry me off? Drop me from the sky? Pick my bones clean? There were so many of them, raucous and chaotic like a wild, windy thunderstorm or powerfully rattling tornado, beautiful and mesmerizing, but also potentially murderous.

My mind, as always, turned to fear. I tightened inside, braced as usual for something bad. And then a moment of remarkable clarity. I had the power to choose my interpretation. Sinister omen or wondrous revelation? Fear or awe? I chose the latter.

And in that instant the blue sky seemed suddenly wilder and extraordinary, shimmering. The air throbbed. The trees quivered. I closed my eyes to absorb the starlings' majestic earthquake presence overhead. The enthralling din enclosed me, surreal and eerie, but also strangely reassuring. I joined their world for a moment, as they had apparently joined mine.

Then in a flash, all together, as if on cue, they emptied the branches as quick as they'd filled them. A great rumbling shook the world as thousands of wings beat simultaneously and shiny black bodies soared out of the treetops in ballet unison to flood the sky. I hadn't heard their signal, but it had arrived, invisibly, in an instant of miraculous instinct.

I've since learned it's called a murmuration. A lovely word for the lustrous bird-cloud that swelled and rolled and swirled as one into the heavens like a giant stream of twisting liquid, a single shape-shifting beast.

Part of me wished I could grow great black wings and murmurate with them. *Come with us. Feel your place in the grand rhythms of the earth. Rise and be part of the world's ever-migrating, ever-evolving, ever-moving soul.*

I thrilled at their raw, frenetic outpouring of joy and freewheeling abandon. They were who and what they were, on an audacious journey without fear or apology. They followed their callings and called what they felt. This was their parade. Just for me, a spectator of one.

And then they were gone. Calm blue and silence returned. Something stagnant was flushed out of the air and out of me. It was a moment of magic. A shift from fear to certainty that I'm more than what's seen, part of something sublime. We all are.

The starlings had stopped to watch my parade, and I ended up watching theirs. But these weren't parades at all. They were pilgrimages. I know that now.

My walks have always been marches into the wild heart of the world to gather inspiration, the place where creations arise and life is formed. I wander to feel the guiding embrace of grace and things greater than me. So do the starlings.

I'd lost my way, but in truth, I'd never really found it. I was still searching for a way to shine with my full toolbox of emotions and talents and share from my most submerged places. The ideas for my creations were mostly directed by others, their bones and guts mostly fashioned from the works of courageous pioneers.

A lucky few seem born to circumvent this struggle, grasping early their connection to things, like my starlings, that know no bounds and have no doubts. I had yet to dig creations out of the messy, authentic center of myself, forever hesitating to lay bare the odd bend of my mind, nerves and heart for fear the world would laugh.

The starlings had invited me to stop and see. They hollowed out a wild place inside me, cleared my path for something sweet and ancient—and bolder—to flow in. They showed me their unabashed artistry, how to live and fly in harmonious unity, guided by the perfect choreography of an unseen force. They swooped and skimmed fearlessly together through a world reverberating with life and energy, form and spirit, where anything can happen if you choose to grab hold.

Trust what you know. Follow life's deepest cues and cadences. Never doubt the air will catch your wings perfectly and transport you in a dance of splendid flight.

Our pilgrimages are the same, mine and theirs. All life's pilgrimages are. We wander for the thrill of magical murmurations, a feeling of oneness, synchronicity and creative joy that my shiny friends dwell in all the time, and I hope to dwell in more.

SIDNEY STEVENS holds an MA in journalism from the University of Michigan and makes her living as a freelance writer. She has contributed essays to *Newsweek*, *Chicken Soup for the Soul*, and *New Works Review*. As a journalist, she specializes in nature and environmental writing. Her articles have appeared in *Sierra Magazine*, as well as on websites including Mother Nature Network and GreenYour. When Sidney is not working, she enjoys creative writing, yoga, making mosaics, reading, traveling, community environmental education, and hiking (which led to her murmuration experience).

Thinking Fox

by Sharona Muir

One spring morning, standing on tiptoe, I peer inside a gap in a hollow ash tree and find a clump of little bodies crying softly, like a teakettle set to simmer. A head is raised, with a minute snoot. A tiny tail has a white point, the sign of a red fox. Among the tree's roots, three holes—a den's exits—suggest that after heavy rains, a vixen brought her pups out of their flooded den to this high nest. Red foxes do not climb trees. She must have leaped and pulled herself over the gap's lip, carrying the pups in one at a time. I wonder how many leaps it took, and whether, the first time, she imagined the arc that would take her within clawing distance of the gap.

I cannot know her thoughts, yet it's irresistible to try. Tradition, stretching from Chinese fox spirits to European folktales to Native American myths, shows that people everywhere have brooded over the tricky minds of foxes. In a poem by Ted Hughes, "The Thought-Fox," a writer sits before a typewriter, while outside, a fox steps delicately through the woods. Finally, the fox leaps into the writer's head, and the writer, inspired, starts banging away on the typewriter.

Foxes don't merely symbolize thought, though; nor do they mean the same to us as other thinking beasts. They are not a pocket edition of the wolf's fierce intelligence or the coyote's street smarts; they are somehow essential. I don't know how to express this, except that once the vixen enters my life, like the writer in Hughes's poem, I can't help thinking fox. I'm thinking that the lint-colored pups, atremble on their spidery claws, were brought here by a fox's leap of faith.

Where will she move? The pups can't stay in the tree. It isn't long before fresh dirt appears around a hole leading under my barn. My husband mounts a motion sensor camera nearby. We're fascinated when the downloaded images reveal ears that poke like petals from the ground—then the pups, pouncing out. The vixen has installed her offspring under the noses of the most feared creatures in our woods. We do keep the other bad guys off; and I'm not alone in thinking that's how she thinks. A researcher at the Ohio Department of Natural Resources, cited in *The Columbus Dispatch,* explains that as the numbers of coyotes rise in the state, foxes are choosing to live near humans for protection from the larger canid. It all adds up. The vixen believes in smart risks.

We don't see much of her. An orange smudge against a tree, gone like smoke. Snapshots show a rump and a blur of legs. Whenever the camera clicks, or lights up, she runs. Living by the camera, observing its activity, she takes nothing for granted. I start wondering if that might be the secret of smart risks. Maybe I'm in a useful fable with this fox.

True to the fables, a dead chicken appears in the den mouth. When prodded, the feathered lump jerks deeper into the hole, emitting the miniature snarls of the pups. It seems that the vixen killed a fowl half her size, then hauled it from the farm a quarter of a mile away, negotiating a barbed-wire fence, a Great Pyrenees shepherd dog, and the local coyote pack. For nights afterwards, we hear the Great Pyrenees' gruff barks, impossible not to anthropomorphize as a disgruntled cop's, "You! I know you're there. Step away from the chickens." Rabbit fur and the feathers of blue jays, doves and whippoorwills also turn up in the den mouth. The vixen is using quite a range of hunting skills and is passing them on to her pups.

After a rainfall, opening my front door, foot poised over the woven raffia doormat, I see—a lucky second before my foot falls—a gutted rabbit stretched across the mat, gray hide baring a red spine. The vixen was thinking about storage in wet weather. She didn't lay the rabbit down randomly on the covered porch. She used my doormat for a drying rack and me for a guard. It's a smart solution. It's also damned chutzpah.

"Faith" isn't an attribute of foxes, according to a 13th century bestiary I've consulted, a curious book that tells a lot of what my husband calls whoppers. Of course, most fables are whoppers, but the best ones reach truth. My bestiary insists that foxes deceitfully play dead in order to trap birds. Okay, they eat birds. Then the Bible is thrown at them: Psalm 63:10 says, *those who seek my soul, to destroy it, shall go into the lower parts of the earth … they shall be a portion for foxes.* To conclude on this basis that a fox—in particular, my risk-taking, hardworking vixen—represents the devil, does not ring true. No, in my book the fox takes a leap of faith that starts the fable. But how it will end, and with what moral, I wait to see.

The pups love to play; they grab each other's tails and pretend to eat each other's heads. (My aunt once had a red fox stole. It looked just like the pups when they nap together on a rock.) Eventually, the chicken bones are recycled as chew toys. They turn up in photos. One day, when the foxes are either not at home or are watching from a safe distance, I go to see the bones themselves. They lie like tossed game counters. The famous thieving of the fox. Now I'm in a fable where everything—my running shoes, the feet inside them, my straw hat, hair, ten-pound head, and the thoughts inside it—is stolen from me in the night, and eventually recycled.

Later in the year, a midwinter night arrives, moon behind clouds. We're wheeling our dumpster up to the road, for trash collection. We wear strap-on headlamps that beam into the bare woods. Four green points of light suddenly come bouncing toward us in a foxy rhythm. My husband grasps my arm; we catch our breaths. Foxes run from humans—but not these! They're headed straight for us! Then they veer, skimming through arcs of darkness, invisibly leaping. It's their mating season. Now it's not a camera registering the vixen's presence, but my body. I call silently to her. You crazy girl! You madcap toiler in the lunar dark! And the eyes of the soul shine back in mine.

SHARONA MUIR's prose has been published in *The New York Times, Granta, Orion, Kenyon Review, Michigan Quarterly Review, ISLE,* and many other journals. Her most recent book, *Invisible Beasts: Tales of the Animals That Go Unseen Among Us* (Bellevue Literary Press, 2014) was a finalist for the Orion Prize. Her work has received the National Endowment for the Arts Fellowship, the Hodder Fellowship from Princeton University, and two Ohio Arts Council Fellowships.

The Daily Pond Walk

by Nancy Canyon

Last summer, Scudder Pond mostly dried up, leaving shallow puddles of chocolatey brown mud, gooey and oozing. At the deep end, the remaining water turned stagnant. Mosquitos swarmed and flies came out. Aphids teemed in the fertile air. The bats arrived.

Now, with spring rains filling Scudder to overflowing, the border of spent reeds surrounding the pond flushes out with fresh sheaths of green. Red-winged blackbirds call *akalee, akalee* and swoop, landing on matted tufts of cattail fluff. The bullfrogs, with their booming *harrumph*, haven't called since last July, but smaller frogs can be heard plopping into the water, shrieking like children as the dog and I pass.

The man with the white beard, whom I often see riding an old bike along the path, pointed out the opening in the reeds last fall—*the den where the beaver family lives*. I'd nodded with interest, imagining walking through the shallow water in my wellies, squishing up to the den and peering in, snooping on their cozy home. Now I stand at the edge of the pond, searching the dark opening from shore, wishing for a glimpse of a beaver. When I see the water ruffle, my heart leaps. But, it's just a turtle diving in from where he's been sunning himself on the muddy bank. Though disappointed, I remind myself that I've already seen one of the beavers swimming about. One day I caught it grazing on meaty lily pads. Quietly I pulled out my phone camera and shot several photos. It was too far in the distance to distinguish clearly, but still, I did see it.

The lilies are filling in now, flat purple-green in morning light, yellow-green in the evening. On rainy days, the pads appear more lavender than purple. Sometimes even pink. On days like today when the sky is rattled and black clouds drift in from the east, crowding the blue patch my mother-in-law said was large enough to make a pair of sailor's pants, the lilies turn somber green. And the wood ducks, with their soft twitter, paddle around feeding: brilliant males wearing patchworks of brown and blue and tawny feathers edged in white. And their smaller female companions wearing black with white eye-patches and beige-speckled under-bellies. Often, when the dog and I approach, the ducks lift off, water spraying, wings beating, the shape of their bodies mimicking the hourglass shape of ducks in old oil paintings—lean bodies, elongated silhouettes flying against a deep blue sky. Today my breath catches: ducklings follow a hen. They run across the flat lily pads blocking their way, then jump into the water, paddling fast to catch up with their mother again.

When I walk the dog, I'm no longer venturing into the world as my planning self, the self who worries, prepares, seeks solutions, writes emails, notes dates and times, lists the things I need to do, and sometimes feels anxiety, frustration, and depression over it all. Instead, I'm wandering the path with my eyes wide in appreciation, breath quickened, senses alert, the summery scent of cottonwoods bringing back memories from childhood summers spent at my grandparents' lake place.

Worries drift as I enter the park. In one hundred feet or so, I'm standing beside the pond, breathing deeply the sweet-smelling air. I become part of the pond and its red-winged blackbirds, rabbits, squirrels, frogs, ducks, and deer. The numerous shades of green, ochre, and blue drain the tension from my shoulders and chest.

Nature's *Healing Spirit*

Twining plants, with their round stems and heart-shaped leaves, shoot up around me. Fresh lily pads reach through the surface, unfurling thick leaves to reflect the sun, and new cattails green-up old papery vegetation.

The first people dug cattail roots, dried them by a fire and pounded the starchy tubers into flour. I remind myself of this fact, and how these reeds also filter the water, removing toxins: fertilizers and soapy detergents and chemicals that contaminate by way of storm drains. The lovely reeds with their velvety tops soft as deer antlers are amazing filters for all kinds of spoilers. The pond is always curing itself, as it does me: clearing negative thoughts, rinsing away worries, evaporating tension, and breezing peace into my life.

Yesterday, a large buck stepped out of the woods and my dog stopped, perking her ears, standing at attention beside me. We watched as the man from the group home, the one who's looking better than he did a year ago, walked toward us. Behind him, the large buck stood frozen in dappled light, eyes unwavering from our small group. I've never spoken to this man before, but when I pointed and said, "Look behind you," he stopped and turned, watching the animal watching us.

He turned back and said, "I heard it, but thought it was a dog coming out of the woods." I smiled. He smiled and walked on.

The buck leapt back into the woods and my dog and I continued our morning stroll, both filled with lightness. I'd connected with the gentleman from the neighborhood home, which somehow made me feel connected to the greater whole. And the dog, well, she was beside herself with anticipation as we neared the deer path.

As we passed the pond, the water mirrored cumulus clouds above, white puffs reflecting off a serene surface. A hummingbird buzzed toward the path and arced back up. I shaded my eyes and watched, noting the color of the sky beyond: peachy. I imagined this color would become a pleasing new addition to my artist palette.

Like the dog on her nose sniffing tall grass, I attune myself to nature. Pulling out my camera phone, I take a photo of a brilliant yellow lily flower just beginning to open. Another shot captures curled pads, unfurling in muted purple tones. My camera is full of pond pictures: here's the pond when the ice covered it; here's the pond after a hard rain; here's the pond when the wind careened up-valley.

The pond stimulates my creativity. I study the photos in my studio, making sketches for new paintings. I recall the reflected light, the fresh air, scampering rabbits and squirrels, the trill of bird songs, and the connections I make with fellow walkers.

One evening recently, while my husband and I walked the dog, we were startled by what sounded like a large boulder being dropped into the pond from high above. We turned to see concentric rings ripple out from near the entrance to the beaver den. A beaver had slapped the surface with its large tail—a warning shot—but there was no sign of the creature. Though we watched for some time, we decided at last that the animal wasn't going to show itself.

We turned back to the path and a wood duck couple flushed from the reeds. While watching them fly into the purpling evening sky, a red-winged blackbird flew at eye level toward us, veering like a crop-duster at the last moment. Then a hummingbird zipped past. We laughed, smiling at each other just as a bat swooped across the path.

My husband laughed, saying, "It's wild out here."

The pond is immediate, the slowness of its life cycle clearing my head of chaos, stimulating my senses, relaxing my being. As Thoreau said, "An early-morning walk is a blessing for the whole day." And, perhaps a late evening walk to bracket the day is also in order, like a shower before bed.

NANCY CANYON is the author of *Saltwater*, a book of poetry, and *Dark Forest*, an e-book of short fiction. Her book, *The Daily Artist: Day-By-Day Prompts for Your Art Practice* is forthcoming from Two Sylvias Press in 2018. Canyon holds the MFA in Creative Writing from Pacific Lutheran University. She lives with her husband near Scudder Pond in Bellingham, Washington, and paints and teaches writing in her Historic Fairhaven Studio. For more see: canyonwriter.blogspot.com and nancyloucanyon.blogspot.com

Mutant Mother

by Susan Hoffmann

I remember that weekend in La Jolla, at my friend Maria's time-share. We were sitting outside, enchanted by the night sky. Ancient stars pierced the urban haze while nervous helicopters and small planes darted back and forth, their flashing lights dancing along the crest of the waves. I don't remember why this jumpy spectacle brought up a drama of my own, only that I blurted out, "It's my fault."

"How can you feel that way?"

The sound of the waves, crashing wildly, interrupted my thoughts. I heard them breaking to my left, out of sight, others to the right. Variations on a theme of waves crashing, I thought, like a piece of music. If the light was just right, I could see them gathering in the distance, plotting their deliberate path to the shore, where they stretched, like a blanket, across the smooth sands of the beach.

"My son's disabled because of me," I continued. "And it's my fault, my bad genes. I'm a mutant mother."

She walked inside, to get a pad of paper. "I'll explain it," she said, sighing with each step. I sat still, as the rhythms of the sea began to comfort me. Here was the end of a journey I'd been stumbling along for nearly 15 years, ever since my son was diagnosed. I had been looking for an answer to the nagging question: *How can a mother make sense of being a carrier of a disabling disorder?* The waves had a message, but I wasn't ready to understand it, at least not initially. First, I had to follow the path laid down by science.

Harrison was born in 1986, healthy and normal by all measures. As a toddler, he could hit a baseball like a pro and laugh his way through any activity. I can still see that impish grin smiling through a layer of spaghetti he'd smeared all over his face. Maybe we let his infectious energy distract us from what others sensed, that he was late to talk and had difficulty making friends. Teachers, parents and even members of my own family whispered their suspicions that Harrison was poorly behaved, the product of bad mothering. It hurt, being the focus of gossip and criticisms, especially when no one yet knew if anything was wrong. That changed in 1993, when DNA testing identified the presence of fragile X syndrome, an inherited chromosomal disorder. He began special education classes and we began—his dad, older brother, and beleaguered mother—to make our way through uncharted waters.

With the diagnosis, I looked everywhere—in journals and books and online sites—for information and any reason to hope for a cure. This search landed me, in 2004, on the web page of Stanford's School of Medicine. Their Behavioral Neurogenetics Research Center was recruiting children, ages 18 months to 18 years, for a study on the effects of this disorder on brain development and function. They would use magnetic resonance imaging (MRI) as well as standard intelligence and behavior tests. "The knowledge gained through this type of research holds promise in helping to develop more refined treatments as well as improved education for children and adolescents with fragile X." The optimistic tone fueled my interest.

I wanted Harrison to participate. I wanted to learn more about fragile X. I allowed myself to imagine a cure, even if Stanford wasn't promising one. And I wanted to assuage my guilt. It was my flawed genes that caused the disorder. Now I needed Harrison to help me understand how two lives could be so impacted by one flawed chromosome. Offering him up to science seemed a good idea. My husband was a chemistry professor, and Harrison's older brother was heading to Harvard to study environmental science. We were a family that believed in science. But before we decided on this trip to Stanford, I had to convince Harrison this was worth his trust in science, too. And before that, I had to tell him about fragile X.

"Ever wonder why you can't read?" I asked around the time of his 18th birthday.

"No," he responded flatly.

"Well, it's because of something I got from my father and passed on to you. It's something called fragile X syndrome."

"Oh."

He picked at his fingers, crossed and uncrossed his legs. He looked nervously around the room, his faced distorted in a way common to people with this disorder, one eye clamped shut and the other unable to maintain a focus. Doctors call this "non-productive motor activity." I think it's Harrison's way of responding to the mental chaos set in motion by new ideas. He was trying to make sense of what I was saying.

With an IQ of 69, how could he comprehend what I barely understood? But I continued. "There's a university called Stanford. Scientists like your daddy work there. They want you to come to Stanford and help them understand fragile X. Maybe they'll help you read, or help other children read. OK? They'll pay you $100. Will you go?"

"They'll give me money?"

"That's the deal."

"I'll think about it."

He agreed to go, probably thinking this would be a vacation. Our family travels a lot, and he enjoys our adventures. But would his upbeat attitude change when he realized the MRI chamber wasn't a ride at an amusement park? I'd find out soon enough.

We took a plane to San Jose, and drove to Stanford's Behavioral Neurogenetics Research Center the next morning. In the lobby, Harrison sank into a chair and hunched his shoulders. I could see his anxiety mounting. He squinted one eye, folded his right hand over his ear, dropped his head to his chest, and started a private, personal conversation. "I've made up my mind," he mumbled. "I won't do it."

Just then, the project manager walked in. She looked at Harrison and quickly threw a concerned glance at me. I suspected she had seen young people like my son, gripped by the discomfort of not knowing what was going on. Would he sign the forms, we both thought, giving his consent? He was 18 and had the legal right to refuse.

"Hello, Harrison," she said. "I'm so happy you're here."

"I won't do it," he said, as much to himself as to her.

The project director and I tried every argument. At one point, I added in a reference to his dad and brother, both in the sciences, and the importance of their work and the work of Stanford scientists.

"I won't do it," he repeated.

When it seemed our efforts would fail, a college student about his brother's age approached us. He was from India, we later learned. His warm dark eyes and calm demeanor suddenly changed the mood. He smiled at Harrison, reached out his hand, and said, "Hey, Harrison. I'm Sud. Ready to go?"

"Suds?" Harrison asked, adding an extra "s" to his name. "Like the soap?"

"Yup," Sud said in perfect American vernacular. "No one could pronounce my Indian name, Sudharshan. Somebody came up with the name Sud and now that's what my friends call me. You can call me Sud, too."

That was good enough for Harrison. He signed the papers and

walked out the door with a young man he now called Suds.

I joined them later in a nearby building where the specially adapted MRI machine filled a huge room. One of Sud's colleagues showed me the adjacent waiting room. It had a window that allowed me to see Harrison, who had already lain down on the table and entered the MRI chamber.

The MRI roared to life, banging to an insistent, unrelenting rhythm. There was a whining sound, too, which set my nerves on end. Was Harrison being subjected to the same misery?

"Is this a cat or a dog?" Sud asked. Harrison looked at a video screen inside the chamber and listened to questions through his earphones. His responses identified which parts of the brain were functioning normally.

"Harrison, is this sound higher or lower than the one before?" I wondered what Harrison was hearing. If it was the same grinding sounds of the MRI echoing in my head, could he really articulate degrees of horrible and irritating in terms of high or low?

"What's that?" Sud asked. "Can you get out? ... No... . If you do, we'll have to start over, and it will take even longer."

I could only hear Sud. But with every pause, I knew Harrison had asked something.

"Really? You're dizzy?"

I felt horrible. I had subjected Harrison to what was becoming an uncomfortable ordeal. Why had I thought this a noble thing, forcing Harrison to play a part in science?

The MRI kept whirring, and Sud's commands kept pace. Harrison had been in the giant chamber for nearly an hour. I was exhausted and worried my son was, too. Should I make it stop?

And then it did stop. I noticed the silence before Harrison burst into the room, victorious.

"I did it!" he said. "I bet you couldn't stay in there the way I did!"

Harrison returned home with a hundred dollars in his pocket and a deep satisfaction that he had accomplished something. He didn't comprehend the goals of the scientific study. In truth, I didn't either, at least not fully. Maybe at some point in the distant future, for some other family, Harrison's brain scan would provide useful information. But I stopped believing that science could change the course of his life, or our family's.

I packed these misgivings, alongside sunscreen and a bottle of wine, to take with me for a weekend in La Jolla. Maria and I walked along the beach, collecting colored sea glass, watching the antics of the seals and sea lions at the Cove, and then marching up the hill to shop. As the day slipped into evening, we bought some food for dinner and headed back to her place.

Maria and I have been friends for years. Our older sons are the same age and grew up together at school and in the neighborhood. She's a professor, and, like my husband, has a specialty in science. When I brought up my feelings of guilt that night, she moved between being my friend and being the reasonable scientist.

"OK, let me draw a picture of fragile X," she said, scribbling on the pad of paper. She drew lines to represent strands of DNA and circles to indicate mutating cells. She used words I'd heard over the years and never understood, words like methylation and somatic mosaicism. That night, the words swept past my ears and disappeared into the louder, more insistent sound of the waves.

Nearing exasperation, she said, "Look. Genetic mutations are a good thing. They mix things up and keep the gene pool dynamic. They are the disorder that helps maintain order. Think of fragile X as a variation on a theme, a completely normal and useful variation of life."

I turned back to the sea, listening to the waves. Some broke in perfect sequence, I noticed, one after the other in an organized pattern. Others crashed at random.

Disorder in order, I began to consider the role of my bad genes in a new way. Maybe Maria was right. They were like the waves, variations on a theme.

For so long, I had turned to science to explain what I perceived as a problem—and then fix it. Maria had presented a different scientific truth, one that I heard echoed that night along the Southern

California coast. I didn't need to change my son or feel guilt. I needed to change the way I valued his life, and mine.

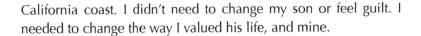

Susan Hoffmann lives in South Pasadena, California, where she writes personal essays inspired by her family. She has retired from a long career in art museum education, having written educational materials and taught classes for the Los Angeles County Museum of Art. She also wrote promotional materials for the California Institute of Technology and the Art Center College of Design, where she taught courses on modern art. Hoffmann's work has been published by *Literary Mama* and *Gravel*. Her essay "A Boy Like Mine" was a finalist in the Tenth Glass Woman Prize.

How We'll Run Away

by Monet Lessner

I am taking a break from my life; driving past small towns and rest stops towards a piece of the past, when my life was like a blank slate of hopefulness. Anxiety grows inside me, tumor-like, killing my appetite and tainting every beautiful thought. Sometimes life is terrible—full of sickness and hard work that leads to nothing. I am old enough to understand this, but the knowledge doesn't help.

Yet today I am the sole passenger on a two-lane highway, with a second cup of coffee and seventy-two hours ahead of me without demands. Dusk sends glares over everything, but I don't want to look away and miss any detail of the glorious view.

To the left, a sudden ravine, and the right, hill after hill after hill, scattered with trees, resplendent even in their thirst. Everywhere the grass grows long and brown and thick, hiding wild things. High, low, rocky, cavernous, covered—utterly untamed.

I spent four summers working here, deep in the south, in Texas Canyon, along the edge of the Frio River. A place where cell phones still don't work and you might encounter a wild pig on a morning run. I traveled this bend dozens of times on days off, tired, but unburdened. Before I knew how many thousands of decisions would rest on my own, personal, limited intellect.

To let other drivers pass, I steer onto the shoulder every few miles. Why do they want to blaze by this wonder? I imagine they must not live in cities like I do, surrounded by billboards and concrete; convenient, ugly shopping centers. I am always in a hurry, but won't hurry through this.

I begin a steep incline and nostalgia—that strange, powerful reflex of one's own, particular history—accompanies me for the next ten miles. I remember the self-consciousness of those summers; the need to communicate something concrete and interesting about myself with every interaction.

Most of the time I wished I was funnier, louder, less sensitive and serious. Age and experience have worn much of that need away, replaced by a certain, *"Come what may, I know myself."* Reaching that confidence took years, like the weathered canyon walls.

This physical place was pivotal—all the solitude, ancient rock and running water worked on me, eroding away those layers of uncertainty. Now I know, there are worse things than being different from someone else's ideal.

I cough into the silence, the raspy sound awful. Though perfectly fine now, a lingering illness has left me so hoarse you can hardly understand me; I might not be able to talk to anyone on this 3-day retreat. I might not even know anyone; I haven't looked at the registrar yet. I'm hoping for some familiar faces, but if I spend the next three days nameless, editing pages alone on a hammock, I'll be perfectly happy.

Turning off the highway onto a narrow road, caliche clears my mind. Bills? Dust under my tires. The worries and responsibilities that constantly nip at my feet like attention-sucking dogs (work, marriage, the news, biopsies, dinner, to name a few)—The window comes down and out they go. It's just me and the silence. Signs appear, familiar markers of hot, July afternoons.

I arrive. That smell! Fresh water, canyon walls. And the timber! Outside and in, it carries the same scent. I don't wait to find out where I'm staying. I leave the bags in the car and head to the river. The unfolding scene comforts me.

Along a granite walkway into the rougher brush, down the stone steps, suddenly opening onto little falls and then, *then*, the river itself set against towering rock; where it bends occasionally over a dirt road or into a hidden valley. A canoe rocks, precariously balanced against the dam you can't even care is man-made because somehow it too has become a part of the venerable beauty that surrounds it.

Though I seldom get back to the canyon, this bit of soul-food mysteriously appears in most of my stories. I review pages and wonder *How did that get here?* How many times have I edited out the vision before me, only to dream of walking barefoot through mossy-covered bottoms? Like it's the home country I left and always long for.

You can see the night sky here; on a cloudless evening, sometimes a trace of the Milky Way. It's the land of goats and javelina, rattlesnakes and nutria, deer and mountain lions. So much more than my stilted being; my individual world. I was dipped in the river a self-focused creature and came up wonderstruck by the universe.

It's been almost two decades since my first summer here; my oldest child is entering her pre-teen years. I'm awed and terrified by what is ahead, how her understanding and character will deepen, and her heart expand. But I know it's so often a difficult road that takes us there.

I have a plan for these coming years, when she's no longer comforted by her mother's head on the pillow, kneeling by the bed until she sleeps. Whenever life seems unbearable, when there isn't a chink in the darkness, we'll come here.

A couple of runaways, we'll stay until she, too, marvels at how her troubles unexplainably disappear in a sudden, dusty gust. Then we'll walk down to the water and stand in the cool, ankle-deep currents, surrounded by high, rocky walls, and watch goats impossibly wander in and out of crevices.

We'll hold hands, stare up at the sky above this loveliness, and look into the infinite; our sorrows becoming small, insignificant things without form.

MONET LESSNER is an educator by day and writer by night (when her kids sleep.) Too many of her daily calories come from coffee, which she needs to keep up with her three kids and late-night writing tendencies. This year one of her pieces was nominated for the Best of Net and Pushcart Prize. You can read her work at Literary Mama and Edify Fiction.

Butterfly Church

by Bridget A. Lyons

Here in Santa Cruz, California, winter is the season for Butterfly Church.

Every November, hoards of monarch butterflies, *Danaus plexippus*, set up their seasonal residences in a grove of towering eucalyptus trees. For years they've chosen the same spot on the west side of town—past the big surf break but before the mobile homes, conveniently located within the boundaries of a California State Park. Here, the delicate insects find shelter from the wind and rain amidst the fragrant eucalyptus leaves. The canopy-like umbrella formed by the trees' branches provides a hiding place when El Niño, La Niña, and the rest of the winter weather family take their aggressions out on the central coast.

I visit the butterflies every few days while they're in town. Sometimes I get a bit overwhelmed by my to-do list and can't get out there during the week, but I always make a point of stopping by on Sundays. I hop on my rusty pink Schwinn and, in Wicked-Witch-of-the-West style, pedal furiously down the bike path, clutching my upright handlebars. Along the way, I might catch the bobbing head of a sea lion out of the corner of my eye or register the sharp clapping sound of an otter extricating its abalone breakfast from a rigid shell—if I'm lucky. Two miles of ice plant and ocean spray later, I lock up my bike at the Visitor Center and step onto the raised boardwalk. Signs caution me to keep my voice down as I enter the grove—for the butterflies or the worshippers?—I am never sure. After just ten strides on the planks, I am swaddled as the monarchs are, by the spicy-sweet odor of the non-native eucalyptus trees.

Most everyone around here seems to know that the butterflies sleep when the ambient air temperature is below fifty-five degrees. The monarchs also hide out when it's rainy or windy, so on inclement weather days, the grove is generally devoid of visitors. When the sun comes out and the mercury rises, delicate orange-topped wings begin to flutter tentatively, as if they're gently coaxing themselves back into an uncertain reality. People seem to like watching this part of the daily ritual best, and most visitors plan their butterfly tours around the sun's trajectory in order to catch it. Once the spectacle is underway, the air in the grove is electrified with skittish motion. Numerous jerky-but-somehow-graceful movements break up the sun's rays as individual organisms dart this way and that in search of food, water, or simply the pleasure of free flight. People flock to see this show; there is majesty in the sheer magnitude of butterflies present, and wonder in watching their seemingly effortless motion.

I'm a little different from the other visitors, though. I don't come to see these tiny organisms fly—although that's always a treat. I come to see them sleep.

When conditions aren't right for flying—and very often, they are not—the butterflies rest dormant in the trees. They hang out, literally, in enormous clumps that, to the untrained eye, can look like aggregations of dried leaves. The undersides of the monarchs' bright, orangey-red wings are a rather dull shade of khaki. When the butterflies are asleep, they fold their wings together so that only their drab undersides show. Then, they latch themselves onto other already-sleeping butterflies. These others are latched onto more others, who are latched onto still more others, creating the typical bedtime clusters of hundreds or thousands of insects that look like leaves.

I am captivated by these densely populated pendant colonies. I never cease to be struck by their wily camouflage, their energy conservation, and their impermanence. I am also blown away by the sheer biomass of genetically complex life that dangles above me. I watch and watch and watch these silent communities, even though movements within them are barely perceptible. I return even on cold rainy mornings to sit on the bench beneath the butterflies' favored sleeping tree. There, I inhale the eucalyptus musk until it permeates my alveoli and sniff the pungent flavors carried on the droplets of a recent rain. While I crane my neck back to maintain my upward gaze, I feel the sting of an ocean-borne wind gust and rub my boot tips in a pile of mulch. I watch the clouds get tangled in the treetops, wondering if they will part long enough to arouse the butterflies. More than anything, though, I simply sit with these creatures, emulating their non-doing.

Lately, my inbox has been flooded with spiritually oriented self-help articles about how to "do" less and "be" more. They are all variations on the oft-cited observation that we call our species "human beings" and not "human doings." Well-meaning authors are quick to remind us that it is the rare person who, on his deathbed, wishes he had accomplished more in his short life. I read these articles from time to time, and I know they are speaking to me and my striving tendencies. At the same time, they seem to have little or no concrete effect on how I live my life.

But the butterflies do.

The monarchs model a way of being that I aspire to espouse. When the sun is out, and the sky is clear, they fly. When the weather isn't right for activity, they sleep. They fold their flashy wings and show the world their dull sides. Their metabolisms slow and their motion ceases. To the best of my knowledge, they aren't impatiently checking the weather every hour, either; they completely tune out until the sun's rays tell them to do otherwise. The butterflies make no excuses and offer no apologies for their clumping behavior. "Conditions aren't right to flit about," their actions say, "so we're not doing it." End of story.

One morning, I walked down the butterfly path only to find bright plastic cones blocking my way. Just past me, one of the park's docents was crouched down, blowing into his cupped hands. The sun had come out briefly earlier that morning—enough so that a few eager individuals left the safety of their clusters. Soon thereafter, the wind picked up and blew horizontal rain into the grove. The early risers had been knocked to the ground where their wet wings stuck to the damp redwood planks. Without immediate sun or assistance, they would die there from lack of food and water or from the ill-placed step of a tourist on the path. The docent was picking up each of the over-zealous creatures and blowing on them, both to warm them up and to dry their wings. One by one, the butterflies flew out of his hands and back up into the shelter of the eucalyptus branches.

How like those enthusiastic early adventurers I can be—always chomping at the bit to do the next thing, see the next thing, be the next thing. I want to flutter in the sun, celebrate my freedom, and show off my electric-orange flight pattern, and I'm so often in a hurry to do it. Yet, it is not the hyper-mobile monarchs I come to visit; I choose to commune with the restful ones. The understated, earth-toned beauty of animals recharging their energy stores and congregating for safety is what draws me, week after week. It is almost as though a wiser part of my being knows the kind of inspiration it needs to tap into, and it knows this inspiration is to be found among creatures who move rhythmically with the pace of nature.

This winter, I took more days off from my overachiever's schedule than I have in the past. If I didn't feel like going running or swimming or biking on weekends, I didn't. And, better yet, I didn't beat myself up for it. I tried to adhere to a strictly disciplined writing schedule, but sometimes I disregarded it altogether in favor of a nap or a walk on the beach. On a couple of especially blustery days, I even stretched out on the couch, reading well past sunset. I cooked a little more, talked a little less. This isn't the characteristic behavior pattern of the human subspecies *California Girl*, although

I suspect that it is an important adaptation and survival strategy of the modern genus *Homo*.

I guess we can't always learn lessons from our immediate tribe. I feel lucky to have found some winged companions to keep me in line.

BRIDGET A. LYONS is just another embodied soul trying to savor her trips around the sun while attempting to make some sense of what we're all doing here. She has temporarily left Santa Cruz to pursue an MFA in creative writing in Flagstaff, AZ, where she also works as a writing instructor, editor and designer. In addition to recording musings in essays, Bridget has written one and a half novels, numerous blogposts about travel and exploration, and a mountain biking guidebook.

The Art of Listening

by Melissa Carroll

Growing up if you had told me that one day I would live—happily—on a cattle ranch, I would have erupted in disbelieving laughter. I was born in New York, and knew trees only as the things that punctuated an endless concrete maze.

My partner Ryan runs the small cattle ranch in south Florida that has been in his family for three generations. Now I am learning the names of all the beautiful tropical plants that grow wild here. Now I can read the sky like a poem, knowing which low-hanging clouds spell precious rain. Now, when it does rain, I stand outside and listen to the droplets cascade down in sweet rhythmic taps against the flat green leaves. We are in a drought and this brief summer storm is a blessing. The smell of rain is ripe, earthy, and succulent. As the clouds break open the heat disperses and the air cools. I let the rain wash over me. Ryan and I tilt our faces upward to the droplets and open our palms to the sky, as one does in the gesture of accepting a gift. I am reminded of the old saying: *Some people feel the rain; others just get wet.*

I have never lived so closely to the earth, and I have also never felt more at peace. In my struggle with depression and anxiety for twenty years, happiness always felt so slippery, so elusive. The problem was that I was grasping for happiness in accomplishments, in material success, in other people's approval and acceptance and affection. It wasn't until I discovered that I could be content within myself, regardless of my external circumstances, that I began to climb out of sadness.

In my early twenties I began to practice meditation and yoga. The instant my first teacher met me she said, "You need to spend more time outdoors." She didn't know I was depressed, but I'm sure she could see that I needed to rekindle my relationship with the world around me. By healing my disconnect with the outside world I have begun to heal the disconnects within myself as well.

Around that time a good friend asked me a simple question that changed my life. One day he asked, "How much time every day do you spend outside?"

I paused and realized that, on most days, I was only outside in the interim between two other indoor spaces: from the air-conditioned comfort of my apartment to my car, from my car to the advertising agency where I worked, and back again. On a weekend I might make a special trip to the beach with friends or convince someone to go kayaking with me. But I didn't make time in nature a conscious part of my daily life.

Now that I live on a ranch, I can easily step outside and open my senses to the richness that surrounds me. One does not need to live on a ranch to be present, of course. It is possible to connect to nature anywhere, even in New York, with its own ecosystem and fervent soundscape. But here, the world reveals itself in small and wondrous ways. Some mornings I sit on the ground and notice the dewdrops that have formed perfect globes on blades of Bahia grass. In these moments I am freed from my inner narrative. In these moments I can create space, I can breathe deeply, I can simply observe. In these moments I can truly recognize the ancient wisdom that I am not, in fact, my thoughts. Instead of letting my thoughts run the show, I can become aware of them just like I would witness any other sound or sensation in nature.

I am learning how to listen. I am learning to pause in the middle of a cow pasture and observe the breeze crackle through the palm fronds. I listen to the crunch of my boots against dry Bahia grass with each step. Lately, I've been hearing so many bird calls—the echo of ducks at sunset, the flutter of doves, the cry of the great heron. Have they always been creating such a chorus? Surely they have; I just wasn't paying attention. The acoustic ecologist Gordon Hempton, who has traveled across the globe recording the world's natural places, beautifully says, "In silence, I hear the presence of everything."

I have learned that the birds and the breeze and the green palms that glitter in the sunlight remind me to pause and be present each time I step outside. By turning to the outside world, I can return inward with more crystalline awareness, freer.

It is difficult work for me, this quieting down. It is a discipline and an art form. But it is essential. The old songs of judgment and worry still play in the back of my head sometimes: *you're not good enough, the future is uncertain, worry about ___.*

So I turn my attention to the orange butterfly floating near the bromeliads. I feel the texture of the air against my skin. I check the sky, hoping for more rain clouds to quell the drought and nourish the pasture. I get out of my own head. The old songs fade into background noise, and I remember I can replace them with new songs. I can choose to be present. In this moment a dove sears its melody across the wind.

"Listen," Ryan says. He is showing me how to listen to the remarkable world around me. Doves coo in the distance, over the whir of Ryan's ATV. We are riding around the pasture at sunset to check on the perimeter fences. The cows are settling down beneath the live oak trees for the evening. The sun dips low on the horizon and illuminates the oaks with gold, shimmering backlight. This is the magic hour of the day, when even the scrubby patches of dry grass are cast in golden rays.

Ryan suddenly cuts the ATV engine and hops off. "Look," he says. He is always teaching me to see. There are two small lilies growing in the pasture. He bends low in the stiff grass. "Let's see if they have a smell." His voice is full of awe, and I admire that this man can wrangle a bull and still be amazed by wildflowers.

The lilies are tiny and lovely—a geometry of white and yellow petals. They seem almost out of place amidst the grasses and errant fennel weeds. With a quick glance across the fields all you would see is a wide green expanse. And yet on closer inspection there are so many small miracles hiding here.

I slide off the ATV and kneel to the earth, stick my face right in one small flower and breathe in. At the end of my inhale is the faint sweet scent. "They're so pretty," I say, as grass etches the skin of my knees. "Should we pluck them for the house?"

I immediately rethink my question, though. I recently read the old platitude, *If you like a flower you will pick it. If you love a flower you will leave it in the ground.* And so we will leave them and let them grow wild.

I bow deeply again to the flowers, to admire them, and to be right here in this moment as best I can. This is a genuflection to the sacred dirt. This is the closest I come to worship. What place more worthy than the earth, from which all possibility can take root?

MELISSA CARROLL is a writer, yoga instructor, and editor of the essay collection *Going OM: Real-Life Stories on and off the Yoga Mat* (Viva Editions, 2014). She is the author of two poetry chapbooks: *The Pretty Machine (ELJ Editions, 2016)* and *The Karma Machine* (YellowJacket Press, 2011), which received the Peter Meinke Prize. She has been a Writer in Residence with the National Parks and received first place in the Parks and Points Nature Writing Contest in 2016. Learn more at www.MelissaCarrollYoga.com.

Moose

by Lisa Timpf

the third morning of our canoe trip, cramp-muscled, stiff,
we emerged from the cocoon of our dome tent
into the semi-dark of a misty dawn
shivering from cold and broken sleep

hearing a splashing to the north, across the river,
we crept closer, and saw
a hulking image, as if
conjured out of the primordial ooze—
a female moose, with a calf in tow
humbled in their presence, and achingly conscious of
the twig-snap fragility of silence
we watched, recognizing ourselves
guests, sojourners in their territory

someone stirred
and the rustle of rain-stop fabric
sent the behemoths scrambling to shore
to disappear, wraith-like, into the woods

when I feel closely pressed
by the relentless hum of cars
I think of them
and remember
awe

LISA TIMPF is a freelance writer who lives in Simcoe, Ontario. Her poetry has appeared in a variety of venues, including *Good Times, Aethlon, Third Wednesday, Eye to the Telescope*, and June Cotner's *Dog Blessings* anthology. When not writing, Lisa enjoys bird watching, cycling, and organic gardening. This particular poem was inspired by a canoe trip in Algonquin Park.

Blackberries

by Donna M. Crow

The nurse remembered Mama, the one with purple fingers, who had her babies in July. Those purple, briar-pricked fingers, the first to touch my face, must have left their mark. But not so anybody would notice, not for a while anyway. It's like the disappearing ink in the cereal box that only re-appears in certain light, and it has taken years.

We followed Mama out to the field, buckets in hand to pick enough for canning, making jams and cobblers. I complained about the heat, the briars, the possibility of snakes. Funny how all those dangers disappeared when playing spies, hiding in weeds or climbing trees. I was a poor hand to do any real help for Mama, but I was there. I was convinced blowing real hard would remove the chiggers. My belly filled faster than my pail, but Mama never complained. If we helped even a little, we got credit for it. She bragged on us when Daddy came home from work and sometimes, I believed her myself.

Most times though, Mama donned the early morning path without us, dew heavy on knee high boots, finger holes cut out of gloves, and did more work before we woke up than we ever thought about doing. By the time we woke, the berries were washed and prepared for the next step, and breakfast was ready. I preferred the berries sprinkled with sugar to any cobbler or pie. So, she always saved a bowl out for us to eat while she was preserving the rest for a winter's feast.

On cold mornings, under heavy quilts, when I was reluctant to get out of bed, Mama spread the taste of summer on fresh home-made bread, near a crackling fireplace. Nothing tastes sweeter as your backside warms against a morning fire. I became a human rotisserie, taking such luxury for granted. It's taken years to appreciate the little things. But what I wouldn't give on a cold winter's day for a fire someone else started and homemade bread and jam someone else made. Come December, forget the presents, it's Mama's blackberry jam cake that tells me Christmas is here.

Each year now, near my birthday, I watch the berry patches, waiting for the first black to appear. When it does, I stop on the trail for the taste that tells me summer has truly arrived. And, the marks of my birthright begin to show, one fingertip at a time as I make plans for the harvest.

Though my teenage daughter has only a slight interest in the berry patch, for now, I can see purple stains splotching her memories. I recognize it in her eyes once the chiggers have been washed off and she's sitting in front of a fresh bowl straight from the patch. I see it in the winter, when we are weary of the cold and summer is as close as thawing out a bag of wild mountain blackberries. She is proud of making her own pie. This year, we tried dumplings for the first time. She loved them.

But it's my married son, who has fully reached the age of appreciation and is often my partner in picking. He is becoming known as a great cobbler maker in his own right, maybe better than me. We don't settle for only those patches conveniently located. We have gone deeper and higher and found the fattest, juiciest berries, our location top secret. Once the season starts, we check our calendars for every opportunity to hit the woods.

I feel close to God out there, in the thicket, milk jug cut open in the front, handle attached to my belt, leaving both hands free to gather what is given, using nature the way it was intended. I know summer is fleeting and blackberry season lasts only about two weeks. It's like a fever with me, not wanting to miss a single berry.

I have become a berry-picking machine. I never eat while I pick. Sometimes I feel greedy, though, leaving few behind for the birds and snakes. I do little picking at the edge of the path, where the berries have blackened too soon in the sun's harsh rays. The edge dwellers, rushing to their demise, are sometimes knotty, tougher to pluck and bitter to the taste. It's the ones farther in that catch my eye, make me forget about snakes as I wade deep into the thicket. Only when I become completely entwined in briars, stuck on all sides and one with the vine, do I find what I'm looking for. They are a lesson in patience, having rested beneath the shade of a Tulip Poplar leaf, breathing in the cooler mountain air. The sun's warm rays dancing through the leaves in perfect proportion to the moisture sipped through root straws, a sweet vacation. They are the ones, bigger than my thumb, that fill a gallon jug in ten minutes. They make me reach farther, take chances with footing and fall into holes. They are my berries, put there for me.

I've heard it said, "You'll know who you are, when you know where you're from." I believe I am from the blackberry patch, marked at birth by Mama's purple fingers.

DONNA M. CROW lives on her family farm on the Kentucky River. She writes fiction, creative nonfiction and poetry. Her nonfiction has won awards including the Emma Bell Miles Award for Essay, the Wilma Dykeman Award and the Betty Gabehart Prize. She received the Sue Ellen Hudson Award for Excellence in writing for her fiction, and her poetry has won the Gurney Norman Prize. Her work has appeared in *Still: The Journal, Kudzu, Now and Then, Literary Leo, The Minnetonka Review, The Louisville Review, Blue Lyra Review* as well as anthologized in *We All Live Downstream, Outscapes: Writings on Fences and Frontiers* and *The Notebook* among others. She received her MFA in Creative Nonfiction from Spalding University.

Three White Pelicans

by Stephen Lottridge

The high desert of southwest Wyoming is bleak and nonconsoling. Open, barren, dry and worn, it does not readily offer comfort. No idyllic scenes of rolling leas, abundant, colorful flowers or gentle, rolling hills. No quiet forested paths, no isolated beaches, no sylvan ponds, no refreshing, sweet-water springs. Vegetation is low, scrub and sparse, with the occasional juniper or aspen where alkali water seeps close to the surface. But if you look closely, and search well, you may find pockets of solace. And on that day, my young daughters, Stephanie and Deirdre, needed such a place.

The divorce had frightened and confused and saddened us all. The pain was fresh and sharp. The day had dragged. The girls, Deirdre in her pink dress and shiny black shoes, Stephanie in her shirt, jeans and tennis shoes, alternately screamed, hit each other, squabbled, quarreled, then banded together, huddled anxiously. I separated them, yelled, offered bribes of treats and toys, threatened, and finally gave it up. I wanted to offer some balm, but found no resource in myself. I rattled around the house purposelessly, room to room, as tension jolted through the space and a mute anguish infiltrated every corner.

Baffled, I stopped before the back window, which I had passed a score of times in the last hour. The slanting afternoon sun glinted on the blue, metal swing set and a swift breeze shook the leaves of the Russian olive tree in the parched lawn. I stood, and a boyhood memory popped inside me, a memory of what had saved me as my parents fought silently toward dissolution. I strode into the living room. "We're going camping," I commanded. They jumped, and heeded.

This was not a planned outing, as our excursions usually were. At that moment, we were fleeing. I knew that the great teachings of human history instruct us not to rely on our environment for our happiness. But we were human and we wanted to escape, outdoors. We loaded the car in a frenzy, exhilarated to be setting out, looking forward with no plan, but on the move. I flung the tent, sleeping bags, pads, back-packing stove and some warm clothes into the back. The girls dragged out sweaters, blankets and their favorite pillows. I jammed in a cooler and the old utensil chest, and we flurried off. Quick stop for gas and ice, another to pick up milk, water, cold cuts, bread, mayo, mustard, fruit, carrots, cereal, juice, coffee and cocoa. Not camping fare, but good enough. No toiletries, just toilet paper. But from years of poking around the arid countryside looking for something hospitable, I knew where we were going. At least I thought I did.

We hit the Interstate west, with coal trains rumbling and semis blasting past, crossed the Green River where Powell started his long exploration of the Grand Canyon, turned right at the top of a long rise and headed north on a two-lane. The girls had quieted, inquisitive and ready for adventure. I had a vague map in my mind of one specific dirt road that would take us back down toward the river. I kept an eye out for it, energized to be underway and uncertain where. Miles along, just as I was thinking I had missed it, we dropped down a steep slope and there it branched, exactly as my memory held it. A quick brake, a crank of the wheel, and a thick dust plume flying out in the southwest wind marked our passage till we veered right onto a faint, hillocky track in the coarse grass that wove through willows and cottonwoods and bounced us to the end of an obscure peninsula.

Rolling to a slow stop, I cut the engine and we tumbled out. Stretching, we heard the sound of ... nothing. No machines. Few reminders of human passage, besides ourselves. The wind still scoured the earth, the grass was sparse and crackly, the sage was prickly, and the cottonwoods twisted and gnarled. But it was as if, in leaving the house, we had come home.

The river rippled swift and even, with a slight susurrus as it swirled through the low grass on the bank. We stood in silence for some time, breathing in the clean air. The faint, slightly acrid smell of the willows, the odor of river mud and vegetation and the scent of crushed sage cleared our heads. Small birds flitted, their quick songs sharp and sweet. Ground squirrels darted and dove.

Tentatively, quietly, companionably, the girls began to explore, calling softly to each other to look at this or that. They wandered together, slowly, one blond head and one brown, hair aflutter, bobbing here and there. My body eased, my eyes sharpened and my ears attuned. My muscles relaxed and came easily alive as I stretched to unpack the gear and pitch camp. The smell and touch of outdoor gear, mine since childhood, gladdened me. I worked steadily, skillfully. The wind eased as evening drew on, leaving a barely audible rustle in the cottonwoods. My tasks done, I joined the girls in walking the land, with no human sounds but our footfalls and our occasional, low voices.

Hunger claimed its own, and we ambled back to camp. Supper was sandwiches, carrots and juice, the tin plates and cups set out on a torn camp blanket covering a patch of lumpy ground. We sat cross-legged, side by side. Some ants joined us, and we shared our food with them. Full, we cleaned up and stowed the food, then came back to the blanket. At the girls' request, I told stories of camping with my family when I was a boy their age, as my parents had told stories to me. We quietly sang a song or two, tunes I had taught them, as the desert sunset spread out across the sky and lit the distant buttes with pastel fire.

We lay back on the blanket as the stars made their entrance. "Star light, star bright ... ." We gazed long, silently, wrapped in our own wishes. The night chill came on suddenly. We rolled over, got to our hands and knees; I herded the girls into the tent and snugged them into their bags. I gave them butterfly kisses, rubbed their backs, told them I loved them and we all said good night.

The girls asleep, breathing in gentle unison, night sounds crept in: the rustle of the running river, the tiny crackle of nocturnal animals in dry vegetation, and the owls, first one, then many, softly booming their calls in the cottonwoods. Images arose: My boss and friend dying in August, and me wandering his house in confusion and terror. My mother, in September, dying in her pauper's hospital bed, her Scottish Presbyterian childhood fear of the torments of hell competing with her adult practice of forgiving meditation, as I massaged her swollen back with blue mineral ice. Her body lying soft and finally tranquil on the gray, metal, mortuary table. My young sister, in November, dying on a distant coast, hair thin, matted, gray, a tube in her nose and catheter in her crotch, begging me to tell her what I thought was going to happen, as I held her bony hand, and pushed aside the flowing tube to kiss her salt, dry lips one last time. My two spinal surgeries, in February and July, as my wife was leaving.

My back pressed against the uneven ground, the images took shape, lingered, faded. Memories of past camping trips arose. I inhaled the familiar odor of canvas, the faint tang of dew-dampened sage drifting in. And the owls, those ancient omens of death, beckoning me. As I attended, sleepless, to their voices, they became warrants of life to me, reassuring, comforting, speaking of wildness, healing and continuity.

Morning found us tousled and cheerful. Yawning and murmuring, we crawled out into the dawn, into cool air and early light. We were quiet. I fetched the food and blanket from the car, put some water on the stove for cocoa and coffee. We dumped Cheerios into bowls and poured milk over them, each to his or her liking. We slurped and chuckled for the fun of it, the spoons clanking invitingly against the speckled, blue-glazed metal. We each poured seconds. I leaned over, sloshed our cups full of coffee and cocoa and settled back between them.

Abruptly, Deirdre said, "Look, Dad!" Stephanie echoed, "Yeah, Dad, look!" In the near eddy, three white pelicans floated toward

us, an adult and two young, tightly grouped, spinning and sway-
ing with awkward grace, holding their place against the current.
The girls leaned closer to me. I put an arm around each as we sat
in wonder. The girls slowly twined themselves into my lap. In the
widening day, we watched silently, gratefully, as the pelicans eyed
us, unafraid.

STEPHEN LOTTRIDGE is a former professor of Slavic Languages and
Literatures, and a retired psychologist. Educated on the coasts,
he is a native of the mountain and sagebrush west. He lives in
Jackson, Wyoming, where he is active in local theater and literary groups. A play he co-wrote was produced in June of 2017.
He has published in *Emerging Voices*, in *Blood, Water, Wind and
Stone: An Anthology of Wyoming Writers* (Sastrugi Press, 2016),
and online through Silver Birch Press. He held the 2017 Fellowship in Creative Nonfiction from the Wyoming Arts Council. Being
in nature has healed him in many times of turmoil and anguish.

Earthsprings Eternal

by Sheila K. Collins

"They're called 'teaching trees' by the natives." My friend Glenda guides a few of us retreat participants on a hike through the Piney Woods of her East Texas property. "Elders use them as examples of the amazing resilience of nature. At our children's retreats we encourage the kids to notice how a tree's trunks and branches adapt to what the wind, weather, time, and neighboring plants and insects send their way."

I'm grateful for an experienced human guide to help us find our footing in the lumpy spring soil. Last week's torrential rains have altered the terrain, but it's my recent health challenge that makes my gait unsteady.

We follow Glenda on the sandy path to exhibit A—a tree whose major parallel branch broke off years ago in a storm. The tree's life force sprouted a new branch that now rises proudly in an upward direction. Not the original intention, but it works out fine. The result isn't as aesthetically pleasing as the original, but I give it extra points for acting on the art of the possible.

Before traveling a well-worn trail to the clearing beside the medicine lodge, we spend a few minutes examining the ropey, hairy vines climbing some of the trees. "That's poison ivy," someone says, and we look more closely at the pointy leaves, greening out from their winter sleep.

This reminder of the danger that lurks in the woods is important for us city-folk used to carefully planned landscapes and temperature-controlled environments. Having spent many summers recovering from exposure to poison oak while gardening in my Texas backyard, I'm also aware that for some highly sensitive people, it isn't necessary to touch the plant. Just breathing its fumes can ignite the negative reaction. But I don't mention that fact right now. This is supposed to be a pleasant stroll in the woods.

Arriving at an enormous grandmother tree we stand in awe. Close inspection reveals that insects are busily burrowing underneath the giant trunk's bark, slowly but consistently pulverizing it to saw dust. Yet her wounds do not define her. The oak tree stands tall, putting out glorious new leaves to the very top of her crowning glory. My thoughts go to the shoulder I broke in a fall a couple of years ago. What a lot of work it has taken to regain my aged body's range of motion, and to again stand tall and straight.

Moving more deeply into the forest we visit two trees whose trunks are intertwined. I'm drawn to these hugging trees. Their solution for survival has been to become stronger as one. I appreciate this implied antidote to the cultural messages that encourage us to rely only on ourselves, as though it's cheating to ask for and give help.

Treading downhill toward the creek bed, we climb in and out of the runoff channel of water carving its way through pine needles, leaves, and sprouting seedlings. Each step triggers memories, taking me back sixty-plus years to the trails of Big Rock Park, a few blocks from my childhood home. The park's name came from a giant boulder the size of a small house that rested on the edge of the creek bed, having broken off years before from the hillside. To reach the rock for climbing we had to navigate the wooded trails on the banks. When we moved to Kentucky the summer I turned nine, every Sunday morning Mother made sure we went to her church. Sunday afternoons Dad took us hiking through his—making sure we'd come to appreciate, as he did, the wonders of the natural world.

The woods became our favorite playground. Dad and my three siblings and I divided into two groups, becoming Davy Crockett and his band of explorers. The first group got a head start to mark their trail and give the second group the challenge of following their subtle cues to a place of rendezvous. If our marking and tracking skills weren't effective, we agreed we'd meet at dusk on the top of the Big Rock.

Here, in the Piney Woods, the group arrives at a familiar spot beside a fallen giant grandfather log. This trunk has been on its side in this spot through all the 20-plus years of my coming to this land. As the deterioration of its wood continues, the tree offers a demonstration of the connection between what Native Americans that once lived on this land called "All Our Relations." Offering nutrients to the soil beneath it, the trunk probably houses snakes and multiple small critters, along with their cache of stashed food.

Realizing we are now in a clearing that wasn't there before reminds me that even disasters have positive consequences. The lightning strike that started the fire that took the life of the pecan tree left it standing mute in the center of the evergreens. Now it provides a useful climbing pole for some ground cover reaching toward the sun. The stepping aside of the larger trees consumed by the flames now provides new seedlings their time to grow in the sun, an opportunity to become the adults in the forest's next generation of full-bodied trees.

Arriving at the spring from which the land gets its name, I take a big breath and consciously release the effort it has taken to arrive. A small statue of the Buddha nestled in the newly emerging greenery inspires me to take out my cell phone and snap a picture. I hope this souvenir will serve as a reminder of this journey from clock time into earth time, this experience of the curative forces of nature, what the Japanese call, "shinrin-yoku" or "forest bathing." I note edible and poison berries growing side-by-side, leaving birds, butterflies, and humans the task of deciphering and selecting what to ingest that could be helpful and what to leave well enough alone. Ah, how I wish I were better at making that judgment in my personal life.

After a long climb up the hill, the wooden rockers on the front porch of the lodge call to me. I pull away from my sister hikers and sit down to rest with a view of Glenda's mother's irises, a glorious lavender and purple field of them. They only bloom in the early spring, and I feel blessed to be here for that short occasion. Started in this place in the 1980s from tender shoots dug up from her family homestead not far from here, they flaunt their resilience. I know for a fact, they or their ancestors have traversed the continent to California and back and been transplanted into many backyards before settling here.

At the blooming field's edge is another hugging tree, one that marks the East from the Medicine Lodge. This tree and I, and the ones that mark the other three directions, have a special bond. Twenty years ago, I selected the base of these trees as a resting place for some of the ashes of my son Ken, who died of AIDs at age 31. Seven years later I added some of the ashes of my 42-year old daughter, Corinne, after she died of Breast Cancer.

Every time I return to Earthsprings, I feel lucky. It's a place in the natural world to reconnect with the past, to become more present to the present, and to dream into the future. A place to consistently remind me of an eternal truth taught by the Hindu Goddess Kali, honored on occasion inside the medicine lodge. Birth, destruction, death, and rebirth are not chaos or punishments for past transgressions, but the natural order, the dance of the universe of which we are each a part.

DR. SHEILA K. COLLINS is a writer, keynote speaker, improvisational artist, and performer. Her award-winning book, *Warrior Mother: Fierce Love, Unbearable Loss and the Rituals that Heal* (She Writes Press, 2013), tells of her journeys with two of her three adult children and her best friend through their life-threatening illnesses and deaths. Using her background as a social work professor, therapist, and performance artist, Dr. Collins demonstrates in her presentations and workshops how art-based tools have helped her and can help others get through life's toughest challenges. Her work has appeared in a recent TEDx talk, When Life Threatens, in *The Examined Life Journal* and in the anthology, *Inside Out: Literature of Mental Illness*. She directs an improvisational troupe, Wing & A Prayer Pittsburgh Players, that assists non-profits in achieving their noble purpose.

Upcoming

Look for more *Nature's Healing Spirit* titles soon.